林语堂
英译诗文选

明清小品

上

外语教学与研究出版社
北京

Contents 目录

The Book of a Cynic

From *Kueiyuyuan Chutan*

Shu Shuehmou

1522-1593

> This man, who was a Minister of Ceremonies, was against
> the whole idea of "orthodoxy" and "orthodox tradition"
> in the Confucian School, believing that the scholars stood
> to benefit by such rigid codification of Confucius's lively
> thoughts and teachings. In particular he was against the
> Neo-Confucianist School—known popularly as *taoshueh*,
> similar in connotation to the word "Puritans" in English—
> believing that it led to great hypocrisy.

The disasters of fire and flood and bandits usually strike the
poor people first. The wasting diseases of emaciation usually
strike at the powerful and the rich.

The best of high officials always ended up with a piece of ugly
writing which sent them back to the country—an impeachment.

The worst of men always obtained a beautiful piece of writing at the end of their days—a eulogy on a tombstone.

If a man has read a great number of books, and does not think things through, he is only a bookcase. One may read through the entire Buddhist Tripitaka, but if he has not a pure heart, he can end up only as a wooden figure.

Be careful not to open your mind to a man of few words. Be equally careful when you meet a man who pushes himself and wants to win your friendship.

A man on his deathbed will yet give detailed instructions, even though he has not much. A retired official will gabble about his days at the capital, even though he no longer holds the official rank.

A man is physically stronger than a woman, but against an aggressive wife his hands are limp. Parents like to maintain their dignity before children, but when they have a disobedient son, they usually shut up.

The world regards those who look down upon money as fools. That is why bribery is rampant. Similarly people who are not accommodating are regarded as "slow stuff" [tardy in getting promotion], and that is why the court is full of yes men.

Clean, fresh writing is like polished sandalwood where the wood grain shows its natural beauty. On the other hand, the writings of the hosts of imitators are like lacquer ware, which shine on the outside but do not wear well.

Do right and do it alone. Commit something wrong and you will need a gang to work with. That is why even a burglar posts someone to watch for him.

There are times when a poor scholar is forced to beg something of his friends, but he will do it with dignity. Even the sages died, but they died with a lasting fame.

When a wife feels unhappy and the husband shares her unhappiness, her unhappiness will vanish. But when a wife gets into a rage, it won't do for the husband also to get into a rage.

It is said that an unscrupulous man can end up as a cabinet minister and the man who has done him a good turn then receives his boomerang. It is also said that an official who owes debts to others must be an honest official. If so, the man who loans him money will feel very sorry to see him lose his job.

If a man quickly gets rich shortly after he gets an office, he cannot amount to much. But if he stays in an office for years and still is not rich, he does not amount to much, either.

A man often talks big to impress people but is a coward at heart. A hypocrite often makes a pretense of sterling honesty but reminds me of a courtesan who refuses to taste food at dinners and then goes home and gorges herself.

An official may solidly turn down big bribes but nibble at little gifts of carpets or coats. That is because the mouse has its own caution in stealing food. Or a man may be honest at first and then grab something really worth while. That resembles a tiger's crouch before the spring.

A police officer may catch thieves with one hand and receive booty with the other. A man may join in condemning adultery but love to take a peep at the adulteress.

Law may be too strict, or too lax. But strict enforcement of law is like screwing the strings too tight, which still produce some music. A general state of lawlessness is like having the strings too loose, when there is no sound at all.

Do not ask your children's opinions when you want to retire, especially the younger children. And do not ask your wife when you want to take a concubine, especially a lately married one.

Man loves woman like one thirsty asking for a drink. Woman loves man like one in a hot climate seeking for a cool place. Therefore the latter stays longer.

A stupid son is worse than a profligate son because there is no hope of a change. A muddle-headed official is worse than a dishonest one because he drags others down with him.

A well-read man often gives opinions from his reading and airs them as his own.

A man whose face changes color at the sight of ten dollars should not be made a mayor. One whose face changes color at the sight of a hundred dollars should not lead an army.

Better try to build up a company of friends when you have money than try to win disciples by your lofty teachings.

Better feed people than bait them with words.

A miser can amass a considerable fortune, but let something happen and he will be like a crushed rat on the streets. A big-hearted man can also go broke, but something happens and he still stays as alive as a centipede who has lost some legs.

A person who likes to drop names can fool the innocent, but not the people with a better background.

Snobbery can be worse among the rich than among the poor. The hatred among brothers is sometimes worse than that among friends.

When you see a man whose eyes are dull and fixed, you can be sure that his mind is gone. When you see a man who is obsequious, look out.

A rash temper can conceal secret greed. A servile, ingratiating appearance helps to conceal emptiness of mind.

Eating and sex follow instincts in which men and animals are alike. Beyond these, in things outside instincts, the truth must be learned through some hard thinking.

If a rich man associates with the poor, he gets a good name. When a poor man associates with the rich, he gets money.

Humility is a virtue, but too much of it bespeaks cunning. Too much silence in a man also indicates a designing mind.

Praise a man at his back and not to his face, and he will really appreciate it when he hears about it.

Wealth and power do not come to a high-minded scholar because he never cares for them and does not run after them. They do come to an aggressive man because he goes to it like an army fighting with its back to a river.

About one third of the book has been translated.

【归有园麈谈（节录）】

明·徐学谟

水火盗贼之害，必先横被于孤贫，虚赢劳瘵之灾大率淹缠乎贵介。

虽贵为卿相，必有一篇极丑文字，送归林下（弹章）；虽恶如梼杌，必有一篇绝好文字，送归地下（墓志）。

心源未彻，纵博综群籍，徒号书厨；根气不清，虽诵说三乘，只如木偶。

遇沉沉不语之士，切莫输心；见悻悻自好之徒，应须防口。

地下无衣食之身，而临绝者犹勤嘱付；林下无冠裳之用，而既休者尚事夸张。

男子之力，必胜于妇人，若对悍妻，其手自缚；父母之尊，素加于卑幼，使遇劣子，其口常嗫。

世以不要钱为痴人，故苞苴塞路；世以不谀人为迟货，故谄佞盈朝。

清虚之作，如水磨楠瘿，自见光辉；剿袭之文，

明·文徵明　东园图（局部）

如油漆盘盂，终嫌气息。

任重道远，取必于身，故为仁由己，当仁不让；随俗习非，必要其党，故奸须用介，盗有把风。

饥寒所迫，虽志士未免求人，但求之有道；患难所临，即圣人亦有死地，顾死之有名。

妇人之悲其夫，益为之悲其悲方已；妇人之怒其夫，转为之怒其怒可乎？

人言背恩者为贵相，则施恩之主坐受其弯弓；或谓负债者必廉官，则放债之人忍见其垂橐。

当始仕而即富者，其人无可用；若终不富者，亦无可用。

乘势作威者，如大人装鬼脸以骇小儿，背地则收下；因事矫廉者，如妓女当筵之不肯举箸，回家则乱吞。

廉于大不廉于小，硕鼠之贪畏也；廉于始不廉于终，老虎之敦蹲也。

一手诘盗，一手窃盗贼，故前盗死而后盗生；一面惩奸，一面窥奸妇，故此奸伏而彼奸犯。

汉法太峻，人情不堪，是柱促而弦危也，宫商犹在；元政不纲，天道所厌，是轸迂而徽慢也，音调何存。

致仕莫问其子，少子犹难；娶妾莫谋于妻，晚妻更忌。

男子好色如渴饮浆，处富贵而能自决裂者，犹有丈夫之气；女子好色如热乘凉，居津要而漫无止足者，是真妾妇之心。

呆子之患，深于浪子，以其终无转智；昏官之害甚于贪官，以其狼籍及人。

明·赵左　望山垂钓图

务博者常被书痴，一挟之，而议论惟知己出。

见十金而色变者，不可以治一邑；见百金而色变者，不可以统三军。

以德感人，不如以财聚人；以言饵人，不如以食化人。

吝者自能致富，然一有事则为过街之鼠；侠者或致破家，然一有事则为百足之虫。

为文而专附带名公者，虽可以佞盲子，而不能博智者之大观。

炎凉之态，处富贵者更甚于贫贱；嫉妒之念，为兄弟者或狠于外人。

目凝而不动者，中必腐烂；言逊而不出者，内有淫邪。

狠暴之性，可以藏贪，柔媚之姿，可以掩拙。

食色之性，是良知也，统观人物而无间；食色之外，无良知也，必由学虑而始明。

素富贵，行乎贫贱，可以得名；素贫贱，行乎富贵，可以得利。

谦，美德也，过谦者，多怀诈；默，懿行也，过默者，或藏奸。

面而誉之，不如背而誉之，其人之感必深。

富贵不随达士，以其无逐尘妄行之心；功名必付狠人，为其有背水决战之气。

Why I Became a Monk

From *The Last Testament (To His Monastic Brothers)*

Li Chuowu

c. 1525-c. 1605

Li Chuowu was one of the most original minds of
the sixteenth century. In history, in interpretation of
the classics, and in discussions of Buddhism, he made
important contributions which were original and shocking
to others. He was among the first to appreciate the novels
as literature. But most important of all, he was a Buddhist
and an outspoken critic of Confucianism, for which he
was persecuted to death. Of a very strong independent
nature, he could never get along with his associates in the
government. Once, on a summer day, he shaved his head
and kept only his beard in order to keep cool, for which he
was dismissed from a magistrate's office. Greatly respected
for his scholarship, he was always invited by friends to
stay with them. He loved to sweep floors as a matter of
cleanliness, and used up brooms faster than his servants
could make them. It was said that for this reason he could
not stand women. He sent his wife and daughters home a
thousand miles away in Fukien while he remained up north
and never married again. On the other hand, his Buddhist

view made him accept women among his hearers when he lectured on Buddhism. Eventually, some ten years after he wrote this *Last Testament* to his monastic brothers at the age of seventy, he was officially accused of attacking Confucianism (which meant no more than that he had independent views of it) and was put in jail. While in jail awaiting sentence, he borrowed a razor and slashed his own throat, and died two days later.

This *Last Testament* is a great document running to about 15,000 words. He left instructions to his Buddhist disciples to keep the rules of the faith and not disgrace it. Running in it was a strong personal feeling like the tone of the Epistles of St. Paul to the churches of Asia Minor. I give here only two excerpts, one being his exhortations to his monastic brothers and the other giving his reason for becoming a monk.

1. Exhortations

When I die, do not send news of my death to my family. For I regarded myself as dead to the family already when I shaved my head and entered this monastery, and wished my family to regard me as dead already.... In other words, my death does not begin today, and since my death may not be regarded as happening today, why wait until my pagoda grave is sealed and then regard me as dead? So you should continue to live even as when I am with you. You should be careful with your speech and your actions, and even more so after my death, that people may say, "The monks of Lunghu Temple really keep the faith, and are worthy to be the associates of Chuowu (myself)." This is the way to please me. Do not grieve because you do not see me any more, because although my body is no longer with you, my spirit is with you whenever you open my books. When you read my books, you shall see my mind and spirit even a thousand times more clearly than even if I were daily with you. Besides, I have this *Last Testament*, which is my agreement with you. Keep these rules of the monastery, and you shall feel as if Old Man Chuowu were living face to face with you, looking at you and pointing at you with my own fingers. For I am so close to you as you are close to me. So grieve not and regard not only the skeleton which shall be all that is left of me as representing me. This I wish you to remember....

You shall keep watch over my pagoda and live according to the rules of the church. So long as Chou Yushan lives, he will take care of you and protect you. Do not be afraid. Liu lives near the city, and he is a true follower of mine, as much as Yang Fengli and the others. Sister Mei Tanjan is born with a woman's body, but in many ways she is ahead of the brothers in her faith. She has taken the holy path and has a firm understanding of the truth and I am not worried. Although she has not formally taken me as her master, it is because she knows that I do not wish to be taken as anyone's master. But she often sent a messenger over a dozen miles to ask me about the doctrines, and I did my best to reply to her questions. She regards me silently as her master, so even though I do not have a single disciple in this world, I could not refuse to answer her questions. In our correspondence, she addresses me as "master" and I also address her as "master." Thus I have not truly broken the rule not to be taken as anyone's master. Is it not strange that she calls me "master" and I call her "master"?

The others I address as "bodhisattvas" who still live in their homes, whereas Sister Tanjan has shaved her head. There are bodhisattvas living in rich homes who receive many visits from their friends and relatives, wherefore they do not have the time and leisure to come together and discuss their religion. They study their sutras at home and often send to ask pertinent questions. These lay sisters cannot therefore be accused of wanting to communicate with me because of my name, and even if lay brothers were to do so, they would be reckoned among the enlightened. They come to me only because they are desperately struggling with the problem of life and death and must ask questions of the temple. You must treat them with respect, for they are bodhisattvas with a female body. There will be some gossip among their relatives, out of love or jealousy. You should be deaf to such rumors and devote your minds entirely to the problem of your salvation. If those who stay at home are steadfast in their search for truth, how much more should you devote yourself to prayer, who are not bothered with the worldly affairs?...

2. Why I Became a Monk

You say sometimes among yourselves that since you have left the world, you are better than those who remain with their families. I have also left the world, but wherein am I better than the others? I left because there really was no other way out. I did not enter the monastery because I had thought that this was a good thing to do, nor because I thought that this was the only way to lead a religious life. Can one not do so at home?

It is my nature that I am impatient of having anyone control my life. The moment man is born into this world, he is controlled by others. Leave alone the period of childhood and of elementary school; even after one is grown-up and in college, he is under the control of parents and teachers and the master examiners. In the government service, he is under the control of his superiors, and when he resigns to return to his home village, he is again under the control of the district and county magistrates and his parents and grandparents.... That is why I refused to return home and wandered all about the country. It is true, I have a great desire to find a friend who knows my heart, but most probably I shall never find one. But I am sincere in this one thing: my innermost craving to achieve absolute freedom and not be controlled by others, and therefore I refuse to accept office or go home. I have not said this to anyone before because it would be difficult for people to believe....

Someone may ask, why do I have to do it here at Macheng, and why did I not do it in my own village? Alas! you would not know the trouble I had before I could bring the razor to my head! When Teng [the magistrate] saw me cut off my hair, he shed tears and told me what his mother said: "I could not eat for a whole day when I heard this unexpected news. You must make him grow his hair again. If you can, I shall regard you as a truly good magistrate and a truly good son to me." Indeed it was not easy for me to become a monk.... Do not regard entering a monastery as a good thing and lightly receive alms and contributions from the people. My throat tightens when I write these words. Alas! I ran into so many troubles in my life and went through such sufferings because I wanted to be just myself. All the ink of the universe will not suffice to record what I suffered....

Coda

I have written the Six Sections in this agreement with you, and in the last section, where I pour out my troubles, you see that I have not tried to spare myself. I have begged you not to weep over me at my death, but here once more I have written so sadly, for I could not help myself. I want you not to feel sorrowful, yet I want you also to feel this sorrow in my heart. For this is true sorrow and true sorrow cannot be stopped. Who can stop it?

Self-Written Epitaph

He was narrow and impatient in his character, haughty in his manners, vulgar in his language, and eccentric in his mind. He had very few friends, but when he met people he put on a cordial expression. He loved to criticize others' faults, and disliked what was good in them. In his hatred of people, he severed his connections with them and continued for life to think of ways to hurt them. A lover of animal comforts, he called himself "Poyi" and "Shuchi" [great hermits]; made of the most common stuff, he declared that he was full of truth and virtue. He would not give a cent to a fellow man under the cover of imitating Yushin [a retired saint farmer], and would not lift a finger to help others in the name of Yang Chu [the philosopher of egotism]. His actions did not match his words, and he could not get along with anybody. Therefore all the people of the village hated him. Tsekung asked Confucius, "What would you think if all the people hated a person?" and Confucius said, "That would not be enough." It is enough for me.[1]

---

[1] Confucius's reply was that it was not enough that all the people of the village liked or disliked a person for a test of a man's character. The true test of a good man was that he was liked by all the good people of the village and hated by the bad.

明·李贽

豫约（节录）

李四官若来，叫他勿假哭作好看，汝等亦决不可遣人报我死，我死不在今日也。自我遣家眷回乡，独自在此落发为僧时，即是死人了也，已欲他辈皆以死人待我了也。总之我死不在今日也。我死既不在今日，何为封塔而乃以死待我也？则汝等之当如平日又可知也，待我如平日，事我如生前，言语不苟，行事不苟，比旧更加谨慎，使人人咸曰龙湖僧之守禁戒也如此，龙湖僧之不谬为卓吾侍者也又如此，其为喜悦我也甚矣，又何必以不复见我为苦而生悲怆也？我之形虽不可复见，而我心则开卷即在矣。读其书，见其人，精神且千万倍，若彼形骸外矣，又何如我书乎？况读其豫约，守其戒禁，则卓吾老子终日对面，十目视之无有如其显，十手指之无有如其亲者，又何必悲恋此一具瘦骨柴头，以为能不忘老子也耶？勉之戒之！

……尔等谨守我塔，长守清规，友山在世，定必护尔，尔等保无恐也。

刘近城是信爱我者，与杨凤里实等。梅澹然是出世丈夫，虽是女身，然男子未易及之，今既学道，有端的知见，我无忧矣。虽不曾拜我为师，——彼知我

明·戴进 关山行旅图

不肯为人师也——然已时时遣人走三十里问法，余虽欲不答得乎？彼以师礼默默事我，我纵不受半个徒弟于世间，亦难以不答其请，故凡答彼请教之书，彼以师称我，我亦以澹然师答其称，终不欲犯此不为人师之戒也。呜呼！不相见而相师，不独师而彼此皆以师称，亦异矣！

于澹然称师者，澹然已落发为佛子也。于众位称菩萨者，众位皆在家，故称菩萨也，然亦真正是菩萨。家殷而门户重，即亲戚往来常礼，亦自无闲旷之期，安得时时聚首共谈此事乎？不聚而谈，则退而看经教，时时问话，皆有的据，此岂可以好名称之！夫即使好名而后为，已是天下奇男子所希有之事，况实在为生死起念，早晚唯向佛门中勤渠拜请者乎？敬之敬之！亦以众菩萨女身也，又是有亲戚爱妒不等，生出闲言长语，不可耳闻也，犹然不一理会，只知埋头学佛道，作出世人，况尔等出家儿并无一事，安可不究心，安可不念佛耶？

……尔等但说出家便是佛了，但过在家人了。今我亦出家，宁有过人者，盖大有不得已焉耳，非以出家为好而后出家也，亦非以必出家乃可修道然后出家也。在家不好修道乎？缘我平生不爱属人管。夫人生出世，此身便属人管了。幼时不必言；纵训蒙师时又不必言；既长而入学，即属师父与提学宗师管矣；入官，即为官管矣。弃官回家，即属本府本县公祖父母管矣。来而迎，去而送；出分金，摆酒席；出轴金，贺寿旦。一毫不谨，失其欢心，则祸患立至，其为管束至入木埋下土未已也，管束得更苦矣。我是以宁飘流四外，不归家也。其访友朋求知己之心虽切，然已亮天下无有知我者；只以不愿属人管一节，既弃官，又不肯回家，乃其本心实意。特以世人难信，故一向不肯言之。……或曰："既如此，在本乡可以落发，又何必麻城？"噫！我在此落发，犹必设尽计校，而后刀得临头。邓眉石见我落发，泣涕甚哀，又述其母之言曰："尔若说我乍闻之整一日不吃饭，饭来亦不下咽，李老伯决定留发也。且汝若能劝得李老伯蓄发，我便说尔是个真孝子，是个第一好官。"呜呼！余之落发，岂容易哉！余唯以不肯受人管束之故，然后落发，又岂容易哉！写至此，我自酸鼻，尔等切勿以落发为好事，而轻易受人布施也！

虽然，余之多事亦已极矣。余唯以不受管束之故，受尽磨难，一生坎坷，将大地为墨，难尽写也。……

以上六条，末条复潦倒哀鸣，可知余言之不顾矣！劝尔等勿哭勿哀，而我复言之哀哀，真情实意，固自不可强也。我愿尔等勿哀，又愿尔等心哀，心哀是真哀也。真哀自难止，人安能止？

自赞

其性褊急，其色矜高，其词鄙俗，其心狂痴，其行率易，其交寡而面见亲热。其与人也，好求其过，而不悦其所长；其恶人也，既绝其人，又终身欲害其人。志在温饱，而自谓伯夷、叔齐；质本齐人，而自谓饱道饫德。分明一介不与，而以有莘藉口；分明毫毛不拔，而谓杨朱贼仁。动与物迕，口与心违。其人如此，乡人皆恶之矣。昔子贡问夫子曰："乡人皆恶之何如？"子曰："未可也。"若居士，其可乎哉！

Letter on the Secret of Getting Along

Letter to Liu Yichang

Tsung Chen
1535-1560

> This is a famous satire on politics. Although the author
> died at the age of thirty-five, he ranked among the "five
> poets" of his day and, which may not appear from the letter
> itself, held good official positions.

I am happy to receive a letter from you from a thousand miles
away. I would be very happy to hear news about you even
without the beautiful gifts which you sent me. I do not know
how to thank you. The sentiments of the letter indicate that
you, as my elder, have not forgotten me and know that I have
been thinking of you quite often.

As for what you say about "getting along with superiors and
inferiors" and showing "competence at the job," I do want to say

something. I know my incompetence already, but am even more conscious of the difficulty of getting along with people.

How do people try to get along these days? Day and night a man in the government would go on horseback and call on the influential people. He reaches the house of an important minister and sees the concierge. The concierge purposely makes it difficult for him to get an interview with the high personage. So he uses honeyed words and exercises his charms like a woman on the concierge, and gives him a tip. While the concierge goes in with his card, he is not asked to go in and is kept waiting. He stands at the stables with the horses and drivers, suffering the awful stench, but he would not think of going away even if he was suffering from cold or hunger or intense heat.

About dusk, the man who took his tip comes out and reports that His Excellency is tired and will not see any more guests today. Will he come tomorrow? That night he takes a nap in a sitting position without undressing and gets up as soon as he hears the cock-a-doodle-doo. He washes up, dashes over on horseback, and knocks at the gate.

"Who is it?" asks the concierge angrily.

"It is I, the caller who was here yesterday."

"Are you out of your mind?" asks the concierge more angrily still. "How do you expect His Excellency to get up so early to receive guests?"

The man swallows the insult and pleads, "Anyway I am here already. Won't you please let me in?"

The concierge gets another tip and he opens the gate and lets him stand at the stables.

If he is lucky, the high personage will send for him. He shuffles forward across the yard with his head properly bent.

"Come in," says the host.

He bends and bows, and purposely stays in that position an extra second. When he straightens himself, he hands over to His Excellency his "longevity gift"[1] of money. The host refuses to take it, but he insists, and the host insists on not receiving it, and he insists again on his taking it. Finally the host sees no other way than to ask his secretary to receive it. The caller bows again, and again purposely stays in that position an extra second. When he straightens himself up again, he leaves with five or six more bows.

When he leaves the reception room, he informs the concierge, "You see His Excellency wants to see me. Next time I come, you must not stand in the way." The concierge makes a respectful bow to him in return.

Greatly delighted, he takes his departure. When meeting some friends on the way, he cracks his whip and informs them, "I just

[1] A euphemism for a bribe.

came from His Excellency's home. I was received royally, most royally." He exaggerates a little. The friends begin to believe that he was royally received and to respect him. The high personage would drop a remark casually: "So-and-so is a good man. I have a good opinion of him." His hearers would agree with him and join in the praise of that person.

This is what you call "getting along with superiors and inferiors." Do you think that I could do it?

I am afraid that I must inform you that since last New Year's Eve when I dropped a formal card, I have not tried to see that high personage for a whole year. When I passed his house, I shut my eyes, covered my ears, and dashed past as if someone was chasing me away. This is my stubborn nature, and the reason I can never succeed in pleasing my superior officials. And the worst about it is that I don't care. I have often said to myself, "I will do what is right in my position and leave the rest to fate." I am afraid that when you read this letter, you will consider me incorrigible.

【 报刘一丈书 】

明·宗臣

数千里外，得长者时赐一书，以慰长想，即亦甚幸矣；何至更辱馈遗，则不才益将何以报焉？书中情意甚殷，即长者之不忘老父，知老父之念长者深也。

至以"上下相孚，才德称位"语不才，则不才有深感焉。夫才德不称，固自知之矣，至于不孚之病，则尤不才为甚。

且今之所谓孚者何哉？日夕策马，候权者之门，门者故不入，则甘言媚词作妇人状，袖金以私之。即门者持刺入，而主人又不即出见，立厩中仆马之间，恶气袭衣袖，即饥寒毒热不可忍，不去也。抵暮，则前所受赠金者出，报客曰："相公倦，谢客矣，客请明日来。"即明日又不敢不来。夜披衣坐，闻鸡鸣即起盥栉，走马推门，门者怒曰："为谁？"则曰："昨日之客来。"则又怒曰："何客之勤也！岂有相公此时出见客乎？"客心耻之，强忍而与言曰："亡奈何矣，姑容我入。"门者又得所赠金，则起而入之。又立向所立厩中。幸主者出，南面召见，则惊走匍匐阶下。主者曰："进！"则再拜，故迟不起，起则上所上寿金。主者故不受，则固请，主者故固不受，则又固请，然后命吏纳之，则又再拜，又故迟不起，起则五六揖始出。出揖门者曰："官人幸顾我，他日来，幸无阻我

42

明·文徵明　溪桥策杖图

也！"门者答揖。大喜，奔出。马上遇所交识，即扬鞭语曰："适自相公家来，相公厚我！厚我！"且虚言状。即所交识亦心畏相公厚之矣。相公又稍稍语人曰："某也贤，某也贤。"闻者亦心计交赞之。此世所谓上下相孚也。长者谓仆能之乎？

前所谓权门者，自岁时伏腊一刺之外，即经年不往也。间道经其门，则亦掩耳闭目，跃马疾走过之，若有所追逐者。斯则仆之褊衷。以此长不见悦于长吏，仆则愈益不顾也。每大言曰："人生有命，吾惟守分而已。"长者闻之，得无厌其为迂乎？

The Enjoyment of Incense

Tu Long
1542-1605

The benefits of the use of incense are manifold. High-minded recluse scholars, engaged in their discussion of truth and religion, feel that it clears their mind and pleases their spirit when they burn a stick of incense. At the fourth watch of the night, when the solitary moon is hanging in the sky, and one feels cool and detached toward life, it emancipates his heart and enables him to whistle leisurely. When one is examining old rubbings of calligraphy before a bright window, or leisurely singing some poetry with a fly-whip in his hand, or when one is reading at night in the lamp light, it helps to drive away the Demon of Sleepiness. You may therefore call it "the ancient companion of the moon." When a lady in red pajamas is standing by your side, and you are holding her hand around the incense burner and whispering secrets to each other, it warms your heart and intensifies your love. You may therefore call it "the ancient stimulant of passion." Or when one has waked up from his afternoon nap and is sitting before a closed window on a rainy day and practicing calligraphy and tasting the mild flavor of tea, the burner is just getting warm and its subtle fragrance floats about and encircles our bodies. Even better still is it when one wakes up from a drinking party and a full moon is shining upon the clear night, and he moves his fingers across the strings or makes a whistle in an empty tower, with the green hills in the distance in full sight, and the half-visible smoke from the remaining embers floats about the door screen. It is also useful for warding off evil smells and the malicious atmosphere of a swamp, useful anywhere and everywhere one goes. The best in quality is *chianan*, but this is difficult to obtain, not accessible to a man living in the mountains. The next best is aloeswood or eaglewood, which is of three grades. The highest grade has too strong a smell, tending to be sharp and pungent; the lowest grade is too dry and also too full of smokes; the middle grade, costing about six or seven cents an ounce, is most soothing and fragrant and can be regarded as exquisite. After one has boiled a pot of tea, he can make use of the burning charcoals and put them in the incense container and let the fire heat it up slowly. In such a satisfying moment, one feels like being transported to the heavenly abode in the company of the immortals, entirely oblivious of human existence. Ah, indeed great is the pleasure! People nowadays lack the appreciation of true fragrance and go in for strange and exotic names, trying to outdo one another by having a mixture of different kinds, not realizing that the fragrance of aloeswood is entirely natural, and that the best of its kind has an indescribable subtlety and mildness.

明·唐寅　悟阳子养性图

【 焚香之趣 】

明·屠隆

　　香之为用，其利最薄。物外高隐，坐语道德，焚

之可以清心悦神。四更残月，兴味萧骚，焚之可以畅

怀舒啸。晴窗塌帖，挥麈闲吟，温灯夜读，焚以还辟
睡魔。谓古伴月可也。红袖在侧，秘语谈私，执手拥
护，焚以熏心热意。谓古助情可也。坐雨闭窗，午睡
初足，就案学书，啜茗味淡，一炉初热，香蔼馥馥
撩人。更宜醉筵醒客，皓月清宵，冰弦戛指，长啸

空楼，苍山极目，未残炉热，香雾隐隐绕帘。又可祛邪辟秽，随其所适，无施不可。品其最优者，伽南止矣。第购之甚艰，非山家所能卒办。其次莫若沉香。沉有三等，上者气太厚，而反嫌于辣；下者质太枯，而又涉于烟；惟中者约六七分一两，最滋润而幽甜，可称妙品。煮茗之馀，即乘茶炉火便，取入香鼎，徐而爇之。当斯会心景界，俨居太清宫与上真游，不复知有人世矣。噫，快哉。近世焚香者，不博真味，徒事好名，兼以诸香合成斗奇争巧，不知沉香出于天然，其幽雅冲澹，自有一种不可形容之妙。

Wish I Had Heard It from an Elder

From *An Teh Chang Cheh Yen*

Chen Chiju

1558-1639

> The writer was a great scholar and collector of rare
> books. He was wealthy and refused office and lived in the
> beautiful rich district of Sungkiang. He devoted his time to
> publishing at his own expense a famous collection of rare
> booklets, the *Paoyentang Rare Books Library*.

A *shiutsai* [college graduate], like a virgin, is afraid of people.
When he enters the government service, he has to feed people,
like a daughter-in-law. When he finally retires in old age, he
likes to give people advice, like a mother-in-law.

There are two sentences that can constitute the art of
government: Act in a crisis with calm, and act during a calm by
thinking ahead of a crisis.

In judging people, judge a common man by where he stands in the important things, but judge a great man by watching what he does in the little things.

Sit quietly for a moment and you realize how you have been foolishly running about. Learn to keep your mouth shut and you realize how you have talked too much. Avoid getting involved in too many things and you realize that you have been wasting your time in unnecessary things. Close your door and you realize that you have been mixed up with too many kinds of people. Have few desires and you realize why you have had so many ills. Be human and you realize that you have been too critical of others.

A member of the gentry always talks about "saving face and keeping regulations." That is what keeps him so busy and occupied. But face and regulations are external things.

How do I know what is good? Anything I do which is

appreciated by people is good. How do I know what is bad? Anything I do which makes people disgusted is bad.

Man conquers heaven. When his mind is set and the vital energy moves, neither fate nor oracles have any power over him.

When there is no news to talk about, the world is in a good way.

A vulgar man always looks for favors and forgets them when he has got what he wants. A gentleman hesitates a great deal before he accepts a favor and then he always remembers it.

Medicine is for saving life, but in the hands of quacks can kill people. Soldiers are for killing people, but in the hands of wise rulers, can save people's lives.

The unbalanced youth who are critical of the older people often die young. This is natural. Since they are critical of the old, why should God let them grow old?

Wang Shaoho says, Confucius warned against love of fighting, love of sex, and love of possession. But these three things are exactly what we share with the animals. Is that why we must be careful?

He who always says that he is right never thinks.

In war, think always of how to save lives.

Forgive your servants when they offend you. Do not forgive them when they offend others.

A man is difficult to know. But a man who is too easy to know is not much worth knowing.

A man who saves up good words as one saves up pennies will eventually be rich mentally.

Do unto others as you would have others do unto you. But

better not expect others to do unto you what you would do unto them.

One must try to be good, but not goody-goody. One must be realistic in understanding the world's ways, but idealistic in one's own motives and action.

Confucianists and Buddhists quarrel and dispute with each other because the Confucianists do not read Buddhist books and the Buddhists do not read Confucianist books. Both are talking about what they do not know.

A reader must learn to stand typographical mistakes as one must learn to stand the ruffians in a market place.

A wealthy man brings few tears to his deathbed because the children are too much occupied with thoughts of the will. A poor man brings many tears to his deathbed because the children love him and have nothing else to think about.

An elderly man does not lightly criticize someone who is really superior.

Beware of a man who is always doubtful when he hears something good about a man, but is quick to believe something bad.

【安得长者言（节录）】

明·陈继儒

做秀才如处子，要怕人；既入仕如媳妇，要养人；归林下如阿婆，要教人。

治国家有二言，曰：忙时闲做，闲时忙做。

看中人看其大处不走作；看豪杰看其小处不渗漏。

静坐然后知平日之气浮；守默然后知平日之言躁；省事然后知平日之费闲；闭户然后知平日之交滥；寡欲

明·项圣谟　松潭听泉图

然后知平日之病多；近情然后知平日之念刻。

士大夫气易动，心易迷，专为"立界墙、全体面"六字断送一生。夫不言堂奥而言界墙，不言腹心而言体面，皆是向外事也。

吾不知所谓善，但使人感者即善也。吾不知所谓恶，但使人恨者即恶也。

人定胜天。志一动气，则命与数为无权。

地方无新闻可说，此便是好风俗、好世界。

小人专望人恩，恩过不感；君子不轻受人恩，受则难忘。

医以生人，而庸工以之杀人；兵以杀人，而圣贤以之生人。

后辈轻薄前辈者，往往促算。何者？彼既贱老，天岂以贱者赠之。

王少河云："好色好斗好得禽兽，别无所长，只长此三件，所以君子戒之。"

只说自家是者，其心粗而气浮也。

既用兵时，全要实心活人。

凡奴仆得罪于人者，不可恕也；得罪于我者，可恕也。

人不易知，然为人而使人易知者，非至人，亦非真豪杰也。

能受善言，如市人求利，寸积铢累，自成富翁。

不可无道心，不可泥道貌；不可有世情，不可忽世相。

儒佛争辨，非惟儒者不读佛书之过，亦佛者不读儒书之过，故两家皆交浅而言深。

读史要耐讹字，如登山耐仄路，踏雪耐危桥，闲居耐俗汉。

金帛多，只是博得垂死时子孙眼泪少，不知其他，知有争而已；金帛少，只是博得垂死时子孙眼泪多，亦不知其他，知有亲而已。

责备贤者，毕竟非长者言。

闻人善则疑之，闻人恶则信之，此满腔杀机也。

漫漫花枝寫更加
晴之春日亭亭好
盈盈弄風洒麈
玉台光采星珠花
眉公 [印]

明·陈继儒　双清图

Talks with a Monk

From *Yentsi Yushih*

Chen Chiju

1558-1639

Read a few more books and talk a little less.

There are people who are completely illiterate but are poets, who cannot say a single *gatha* [prayer-formula] but are religious, who cannot touch a drop but appreciate wine, and who do not know a thing about rocks but have the sense of painters. They are born that way.

I do not know who wrote this "More-and-Less Song." It runs as follows: Drink less wine, eat more rice. Take less meat, eat more vegetables. Shut your eyes more, open your mouth less. Comb your hair more, take less baths. Live alone more, mix in company less. Collect more books, keep less jades. Stand more insults, take less fame. Do more good works, think less of government honors. Repeat not an advantage, and count less on good luck.

Su Tseyu [Su Tungpo's brother] loved to say, "Being often ill is good for studying Taoism. Having many sorrows is good for understanding Buddhism."

Seafood is not salty although it comes from the sea.

There is a formula for enjoying living in the mountains: no trees planted in rows, no rocks without moss, no worries in the mind, no flurries in the house.

When I get an ancient edition, I have it copied; after it is copied, I have it checked; after checking, have it set up; after setup, have it checked again; after checking, have it printed; and after printing, have it checked again. Even with such care, there are two or three per cent typographical errors. In this matter, where the eyes face something directly and closely, there are mistakes. How much less credence should we place upon gossip carried by word of mouth?

The White-skeleton Vision Method [Buddhist]. First imagine that your right toe is infected and has a festering sore; gradually it spreads to the ankle, and then the knee and the waist. The same thing happens to your left leg. Gradually the disease spreads from the waist, the belly, then up the chest, and gradually covers the neck and the head. Your whole body will have decayed and only a white skeleton remains. You should then look at this white skeleton piece by piece, and every piece, carefully, steadily, and long. Then you ask yourself, "Who is this white skeleton, and who is the person looking at the white skeleton? You separate your self from the body and regard them as two different things. Then you gradually see the white skeleton move away from your body, first ten feet, then fifty feet, then a hundred feet, then miles. You feel that this white skeleton does not belong to you at all. Keep this image in mind and you will come to think of your self as different from the bodily frame. We borrow, as it were, this frame to live in merely like a guest, and refuse to believe that it will last forever for us to live in. In this way, we can come to look upon life and death as the same thing.

> What a cruel thought, and what a sad one! Buddhists have taught people to banish their sex desires by looking upon a beautiful young woman and reflecting that she is only a mass of fairly stable bones and not so stable flesh. One can fool oneself, but what ugly thoughts!

When you look at a good piece of calligraphy, see it as if you had suddenly met a stranger. Do not scrutinize his ears, eyes, and particular features, but look at his laughter, his expression, and the living spirit of the man.

Mr. Fu says, "Loosen your belt and do not knit your brows, and you will feel much better whatever happens."

I have translated at random a small portion selected from the book. There is much in it which has to do with artistic appreciation, similar to *Quiet Dream Shadows* and which needs not be duplicated. The process of selection for translation is largely a matter of the meeting of the minds of the author and the translator. Sometimes, in reading a line, the minds meet and the English translation comes easily and naturally. Sometimes one has to search for the proper expression, and then it will most likely be belabored. Sometimes one tries, fails, and just gives up.

There is a whole jungle of such books of reflections in the Paoyentang collection, edited by the present author (better known as Chen Meikung), and in other collections. Chen Meikung himself produced about ten volumes of such notes. I hope I have selected the best in the above two books.

A great many other books contain moralizations or platitudes, of the making of which there is no end. Shut up a Chinese scholar for a few months or a year in prison, and he is sure to come up with a book of moralizations.

【 岩栖幽事（节录） 】

明·陈继儒

多读两句书，少说一句话。

人有一字不识而多诗意，一偈不参而多禅意，一勺不濡而多酒意，一石不晓而多画意，淡宕故也。

《多少箴》，不知何人所作，其词云：少饮酒，多啜粥；多茹菜，少食肉；少开口，多闭目；多梳头，少洗浴；少群居，多独宿；多收书，少积玉；少取名，多忍辱；多行善，少干禄；便宜勿再往，好事不如无。

苏子由每云：多疾病，则学道宜；多忧患，则学佛宜。

海味不咸。

居山有四法：树无行次，石无位置，屋无宏肆，心无机事。

余得古书，校过付抄，抄后复校；校过付刻，刻后复校；校过即印，印后复校。然鲁鱼帝虎，百有二三。夫眼眼相对尚然，况以耳传耳，其是非毁誉宁有真乎？

明·徐渭 水墨葡萄图

白骨观法：想右脚大指肿烂流恶水，渐渐至胫至膝至腰，左脚亦如此。渐渐烂过腰至腹至胸，以至颈顶，尽皆烂了，惟有白骨。须分明历历观看，白骨一一尽见。静心观看良久，乃思观白骨者是谁？白骨是谁？是知身体与我常为二物矣。又渐渐离白骨观看，先离一丈，以至五丈、十丈，乃至百丈、千丈，是知白骨与我了不相干也。常作此想，则我与形骸本为二物，我转寄于形骸中，岂可谓此形骸终久不坏？而我常住其中，如此便可齐死生矣。

临帖如骤见异，人不必相其耳目头面，当观其举止笑语，真精神流注处，此庄子所谓目击而道者也。

傅大士云：宽着肚皮须忍辱，放开眉眼任从它。

明·杨文骢 秋林远岫图

Sketches by the Little Window

Chen Chiju
1558-1639

For enjoying flowers, one must secure big-hearted friends. For going to sing-song houses to have a look at sing-song girls, one must secure temperate friends. For going up a high mountain, one must secure romantic friends. For boating, one must secure friends with an expansive nature. For facing the moon, one must secure friends with a cool philosophy. For anticipating snow, one must secure beautiful friends. For a wine party, one must secure friends with flavor and charm.

Formal drinking should be slow and leisurely, unrestrained drinking should be elegant and romantic; a sick person should drink a small quantity, and a sad person should drink to get drunk. Drinking in the spring should take place in a courtyard, in summer in the outskirts of a city, in autumn on a boat and in winter in the house, and at night it should be enjoyed in the presence of the moon.

There is a proper time and place for getting drunk. One should get drunk before flowers in the daytime, in order to assimilate their light and color; and one should get drunk in snow in the night-time, in order to clear his thoughts. A man getting drunk when happy at success should sing, in order to harmonize his spirit; and a man getting drunk at a farewell party should strike a musical tone, in order to strengthen his spirit. A drunk scholar should be careful in his conduct, in order to avoid humiliations; and a drunk military man should order gallons and put up more flags, in order to increase his military splendor. Drinking in a tower should take place in summer, in order to profit from the cool atmosphere; and drinking on the water should take place in autumn, in order to increase the sense of elated freedom. These are proper ways of drinking in respect of mood and scenery, and to violate these rules is to miss the pleasure of drinking.

In my studio, all formalities will be abolished, and only the most intimate friends will be admitted. They will be treated with rich or poor fare such as I eat, and we will chat and laugh and forget our own existence. We will not discuss the right and wrong of other people and will be totally indifferent to worldly glory and wealth. In our leisure we will discuss the ancients and the moderns, and in our quiet, we will play with the mountains and rivers. Then we will have thin, clear tea and good wine to fit into the atmosphere of delightful seclusion. That is my conception of the pleasure of friendship.

We burn incense on a moonlight night and play three stanzas of music from an ancient instrument, and immediately the myriad worries of our breast are banished and all our foolish ambitions or desires are forgotten. We will then inquire, what is the fragrance of this incense, what is the color of the smoke, what is that shadow that comes through the white papered windows, what is this sound that arises from below my fingertips, what is this enjoyment which makes us so quietly happy and so forgetful of everything else, and what is the condition of the infinite universe?

For such a quiet studio, one should have *wut'ung* trees in front and some green bamboos behind. On the south of the house, the eaves will stretch boldly forward, while on the north side, there will be small windows, which can be closed in spring and winter to shelter one from rain and wind, and opened in summer and autumn for ventilation. The beauty of the *wut'ung* tree is that all its leaves fall off in spring and winter, thus admitting us to the full enjoyment of the sun's warmth, while in summer and autumn its shade protects us from the scorching heat.

Build a house of several beams, grow a hedge of *chin* trees and cover a pavilion with a hay-thatch. Three *mow* of land will be devoted to planting bamboos and flowers and fruit trees, while two *mow* will be devoted to planting vegetables. The four walls of a room are bare and the room is empty, with the exception of two or three rough beds placed in the pavilion. A peasant boy will be kept to water the vegetables and clear the weeds. So then one may arm one's self with books and a sword against solitude, and provide a *ch'in* (a stringed instrument) and chess to anticipate the coming of good friends. This is one of the ways that can make one's old age more lively.

Inside the gate there is a footpath and the footpath must be winding. At the turn of the footpath there is an outdoor screen and the screen must be small. Behind the screen there is a terrace and the terrace must be level. On the banks of the terrace there are flowers and the flowers must be bright-colored. Beyond the flowers there is a wall and the wall must be low. By the side of the wall there is a pine tree and the pine must be old. At the foot of the pine tree there are rocks and the rocks must be quaint. Over the rocks there is a pavilion and the pavilion must be simple. Behind the pavilion there are bamboos and the bamboos must be sparse. At the end of the bamboos there is a house and the house must be secluded. By the side of the house there is a road and the road must branch off. At the point where several roads come together, there is a bridge and the bridge must be tantalizing to cross. At the end of the bridge there are trees and the trees must be tall. In the shade of the trees there is grass and the grass must be green. Above the grass plot there is a ditch and the ditch must be slender. At the top of the ditch there is a spring and the spring must gurgle. Above the spring there is a hill and the hill must be undulating. Below the hill there is a hall and the hall must be square. At the corner of the hall there is a vegetable garden and the garden must be big. In the garden there is a stork and the stork must dance. The stork announces there is a guest and the guest must not be vulgar. When the guest arrives he is offered wine and the wine must not be declined. At the drink the guest must get drunk and the drunken guest must not want to go home.

【 小窗幽记 】

明·陈继儒

赏花须结豪友，观妓须结淡友，登山须结逸友，泛舟须结旷友，对月须结冷友，待雪须结艳友，捉酒须结韵友。

法饮宜舒，放饮宜雅，病饮宜小，愁饮宜醉，春饮宜郊，夏饮宜庭，秋饮宜舟，冬饮宜室，夜饮宜月。

凡醉各有所宜。醉花宜昼，袭其光也；醉雪宜夜，清其思也；醉得意宜唱，宣其和也；醉将离宜击钵，壮其神也；醉文人宜谨节奏，畏其侮也；醉俊人

明·周臣　春泉小隐图（局部）

宜益觥盂加旗帜，助其怒也；醉楼宜暑，资其清也；醉水宜秋，泛其爽也。此皆审其宜，考其景，反此则失饮矣。

吾斋之中，不尚虚礼。凡入此斋，均为知己；随分款留，忘形笑语；不言是非，不侥荣利；闲谈古今，静玩山水；清茶好酒，以适幽趣。臭味之交，如斯而已。

月夜焚香，古桐三弄，便觉万虑都忘，妄想尽绝。试看香是何味？烟是何色？穿窗之白是何影？指下之余是何音？恬然乐之而悠然忘之者，是何趣？不可思量处，是何境？

凡静室，须前栽碧梧，后种翠竹，前檐放步，北用暗窗，春冬闭之，以避风雨，夏秋可开，以通凉爽。然碧梧之趣，春冬落叶，以舒负暄融和之乐，夏秋交荫，以蔽炎烁蒸烈之气，四时得宜，莫此为胜。

筑室数楹，编槿为篱，结茅为亭。以三亩荫竹树栽花果，二亩种蔬菜，四壁清旷，空诸所有，蓄山童灌园剃草，置二三胡床着亭下，扶书剑以伴孤寂，携琴弈以迟良友，此亦可以娱老。

门内有径，径欲曲；径转有屏，屏欲小；屏进有阶，阶欲平；阶畔有花，花欲鲜；花外有墙，墙欲低；墙内有松，松欲古；松底有石，石欲怪；石面有亭，亭欲朴；亭后有竹，竹欲疏；竹尽有室，室欲幽；室旁有路，路欲分；路合有桥，桥欲危；桥边有树，树欲高；树阴有草，草欲青；草上有渠，渠欲细；渠引有泉，泉欲瀑；泉去有山，山欲深；山下有屋，屋欲方；屋角有圃，圃欲宽；圃中有鹤，鹤欲舞；鹤报有客，客不俗；客至有酒，酒欲不却；酒行有醉，醉欲不归。

Mi Fei, the Eccentric Genius

Preface to *Collection of Mi Fei's Sundry Scripts*

Chen Chiju

1558-1639

Genius borders on insanity. Mi Fei (1051-1107), one of the
greatest landscape painters of all China's history, already
won the name of "Mi the Crazy One" in his lifetime. He
once asked Su Tungpo, "People call me crazy. What do you
think?" Tungpo replied, "I follow the majority." While
Tungpo painted bamboos and rocks in the foreground,
with powerful strokes for the bamboo leaves and sparse
contours for the rocks, leaving the background a blank, Mi
Fei developed his special landscapes of distant views of snow
and haze and mountain peaks and sparse winter branches.
Tungpo came to know him quite late, especially in the
last year of his life, Mi being a much younger man, and
then gave him unreserved recognition. He was also a great
connoisseur and devoted collector and spared no effort in
trying to see valuable art treasure. Later he painted for the
emperor and was given the extraordinary privilege of seeing
the emperor's private collections.

Mi Fei earned the name of being crazy because he had a craze for beautiful rocks, so much so that when falling in love with a special piece of rock of unusual rugged strength of lines in Wuwei, where he was magistrate, he dressed up in his formal cap and gown and knelt down before the rock and called it "father-in-law." Once he received a stone of a special luster from a monk and slept embracing the stone for three days. He also coveted the emperor's own inkstone which he saw while commissioned to do a painting, and said to the emperor, "This inkstone has been contaminated by my unworthy hand, and is no longer fit for Your Majesty." The emperor, Huitsung, himself a great painter, smiled and gave it to him. Otherwise he was a very courteous and unassuming person.

When one says that genius borders on insanity, it means, in Mi Fei's case at least, only that genius implies an intense love for the object of his devotion which other people cannot understand. This essay makes the distinction between true genius and mere eccentricity, serving I think a useful warning to people who are merely eccentric without genius. Chen Chiju (better known as Chen Meikung) was a great collector of rare scripts and published an important library of rare books.

When I read *The Anecdotes of Mi the Crazy One* by Lu Yujen, I was dissatisfied at its incompleteness and thought I should try to make it complete someday. The collectors of Chiangtung often take down whatever Mi Fei wrote on his or other people's paintings. Fan Changkang, who is a very well-read man, has collected these and arranged them in a book called *Chihlin* [*Collection of Sundry Scripts*], and has asked me for a preface.

I think there were many charming people in history, but only Mi Fei was known for his eccentricity. The point is that such a name is not easily earned. Behind it there must be a great "expansive spirit" [of Mencius]. Modern people often like to defy conventions and call themselves "emancipated" by being sloppy and disorderly, making Mi the Crazy One a cover for their eccentric tricks.

But is it easy to be "eccentric" like Mi Fei? In the first place, he was a highly cultivated man. He based his calligraphy on the foundation of Wang, father and son, and later was influenced

by Yen Pingyuan [Chenching]. And he cut and he hewed
before he developed his own style. His landscapes were built
on the solid foundation of [Tung] Chuyuan. He did not write
much, poems or prose, but what he did was surcharged with
power and depth. In the second place, he was not isolated but
had the friendship of many great scholars and painters like
Huang Shanku, Tsin Shaoyu, Shueh Wenchu, Li Lungmien,
Liu Ching, and Wang Chinching, who all loved his company.
He was thus able to discuss art and literature and history
with these men and wrote his comments on paintings in their
presence. In the third place, he had exceptional opportunity
to see the best, from the manuscripts of Wang, Shieh, Ku, and
Lu to the original works of Wang Mochieh [Wang Wei]. His
own collection almost rivaled a royal private collection, and
he lived at the Paochin, Chingming, and Haiyu Temples. In
the fourth place, he loved order and cleanliness to the point
of a fetish. He went so far as to wash his ceremonial gown
after attending sacrifices with the emperor at the temple, for
which he was dismissed from his office. This came from his

extreme inability to stand dirt of any kind. In the fifth place, he did not follow the fashions of his times but dressed simply, lived quietly, and did not talk much, nor did he follow the usual social rules. In the sixth place, he was not a flatterer or a snob. He was commissioned by imperial order to write a copy of *Huangtingching* and paint a screen for the emperor's use. The way he laid his brush compelled the admiration of the emperor, who granted him a gift of wines, fruit, and stationery and held the door screen for him to pass. But he dared ask the emperor for the inkstone which he loved. In the seventh place, his eccentricity was not a pose, for in his correspondence when he came to the signature where he wrote [in the usual form] "Fei makes his bow," he really stood erect and made a bow [to the absent correspondent].

Indeed Mi the Crazy One was unique in his times.... He died in his office with the Huaiyang Army. The day before he died, he burned all his works, arranged his coffin in the hall, lighted an incense on it, and sat erect in it. When the time came, he put his palms together and drew his last breath.[1] It seems that there was not a speck of material concerns in his mind. Perhaps he was what the disciples of Confucius would call "an ancient eccentric." In the time of Confucius, the "eccentric one of Chu" was Chiehyu; in the time of the Neo-Confucianists, the "eccentric one of Chu" was Mi Fei. Many can try to copy his eccentricity, but not many possess that gift of the expansive spirit.

---

[1] His last words were: "I came from the Land of Fragrance; to the Land of Fragrance now I return," the words of a Buddhist.

【《米襄阳志林》序】

明·陈继儒

　　予谈陆友仁《米颠遗事》，恨其故实未备，尝发意排纂。江东好古收藏之家所遇襄阳书画，小有题识者，辄手录之。而范长康多读异书，搜讨米事，尤丑类而详，因题曰《志林》，请予叙。

　　予惟古今隽人多矣，惟米氏以颠著。要之，颠不虚得，大要浩然之气全耳。后人喜通脱而惮检括，沓拖拉捞，沾沾藉米颠氏为口实。夫米公之颠，谈何容易！公书初摹二王，晚入颜平原，掷斤置削，而后变化出焉，其云山一一以董、巨为师，诗文不多见，顾

明·陈洪绶　米颠拜石图

崖绝魁垒如深往者，而公之颠始不俗。两苏、黄豫章、秦淮海、薛河东、德麟、龙眠、刘泾、王晋卿之徒，皆爱而乐与之游，相与跌宕文史，品题翰墨，而公之颠始不孤。所居有宝晋、净名、海岳，自王、谢、顾、陆真迹以至摩诘，玉躞金题，几埒秘府，而公之颠始不寒。陪祀太庙，洗去祭服藻火，至褫职，然洁疾淫性不能忍，而公之颠始不秽。冠带衣襦，起居语默，略以意行，绝不用世法，而公之颠始不落近代。奉敕写《黄庭》，写御屏，奋笔振袖，酣叫淋漓，天子为卷帘动色，彻赐酒果，文其甚则跪请御前砚以归，而公之颠始不屈挫。寄人尺牍，写至"芾拜"，则必整襟拜而书之，而公之颠始不堕狡狯。

呜呼米颠，旷代一人而已！求诸古今，张长史得其怪；倪元镇得其洁；敷文学士与高尚书得其笔；滑稽谈笑，游戏殿廷，东方朔、李白得其豪。故曰：米公之颠，谈何容易！公没于淮阳军，先一月，尽焚其平生书画。预置一棺，焚香清坐其中。及期举拂，合掌而逝。吾视其胸中，直落落无一物者，其圣门所谓古之狂欤？洙泗之时，楚狂在接舆；濂洛之时，楚狂在芾。其颠可及也，其浩然之气不可及也。

From an Artist's Notebook

From *Purple Peach Hall Miscellany*
(*Tsetaoshien Tsatuo*)

Li Jih-hua

1565-1635

Li Jih-hua was a painter of the "literary man's" style and a
connoisseur. Most artists have recorded their chats about
art in some notebook or other, but such writing usually
lacks the lightness and joy of Li's work. Incidentally, he met
the great Italian missionary Matteo Ricci, as he recorded
in a small paragraph, included here. All such notebooks
are truly random notes in that the range of subjects noted
is as wide as that of a literary man's conversation, from the
strange and unfamiliar and exotic to the touching and
delicate problems of everyday living. I have selected and
translated here such passages as may interest a Western
reader, particularly those showing insight into an artist's
life and his problems. I begin with a note which touches
on the theme of the following selection describing the
communion with nature of the great painter Huang
Kungwang (Tsechiu, 1269-1358) of the Mongol Dynasty[1],
who called himself "Grand Idiot Taoist."

---

[1] Yuan Dynasty——编者注。

Magistrate Chen once told me this about Huang Tsechiu.
He used to sit in a thick bamboo grove, among rocks and
brushwood, in some deserted mountain. He seemed lost in
thought and people could not make out what he was doing.
Often he went to the place where the river joined the sea,
and watched the tossing and surging waves. He stood there
transfixed, unmindful of howling storms or moaning sea spirits.
Alas! perhaps this is the reason why the Grand Idiot's work has
such depth and power, almost equal to that of the Creator.

The ancient painter Ku Kaichih (A.D. 345-411) painted
portraits and Chang Sengyu (c. A.D. 502-556) painted dragons,
and both did not fill in the eyeball at once, the idea being
that the whole expression depended upon it. The painters of
landscapes regarded the moss like the eyes on a face and spent a
great deal of thought on filling it in. I have heard that Paishi
(c. 1155-c. 1235) had a trunkful of landscapes, all with the
moss unmarked. He said to people, "I don't feel up to it today.
Someday when my head is very clear, I will do it."

A painter must understand give-and-take. By "taking" is meant grasping and sketching in the rough contour of things. Though it is important that such strokes be firm, yet the great thing in such strokes is a lightness of spirit—continuing and breaking at places. If one draws a straight line, it becomes dead and wooden and laborious. By "giving" is meant the omissions, any discontinuity being carried on in space, like the faint outlines of distant hills or the lopped-off branches of trees, which seem to exist and yet not to exist.

Sometimes, walking in the country, one sees a strangely beautiful rock or tree. One should take out pen and paper and make a rough sketch of it. This is similar to Li Ho's method of writing [poetry] on slips of paper and throwing them into his bag.

Let your painting develop like floating clouds, sailing into space and going around rocks, spreading out here and obstructing the sunlight there, with complete spontaneity.

That is the way to achieve an effect of nature. Then it will hold. Practicing calligraphy is like washing pebbles. When the dirt on the surface is washed off, the colors and brilliance of the pebbles reveal themselves naturally. In both cases, the vitality comes from careful observation in spare time and high concentration and mastery at the time the brush touches the paper.

The reason why the moderns cannot compare with the ancients is that they have not the vital force of the latter. This vital force does not come from strenuous effort, as if one could do a piece of creative work just by setting one's jaws tight. Then what is it? The answer lies in this: stand aloof from thoughts of fame and profit and take a cultured, detached view of life, so that one's spirit comes nearer and nearer to that of the ancients. Then one will have taken hold of oneself, and be ready for the discovery of that great world of freedom in beauty.

My disciple Huang Changfu asked me for a handwritten script, and I wrote the following grading of antiques in their order of value:[2]

1. Calligraphy of Chin and Tang.

2. Paintings of Wutai and Earlier Sung.

3. Ancient rubbings [prints from inscriptions] of Sui, Tang, and Sung.

4. Calligraphy of Su Tungpo (1036-1101), Huang Tingchien (1045-1105), Mi Fei (1051-1107), and Tsai Shiang (1012-1067).

5. Paintings of Yuan Dynasty.

6. Calligraphy of Shienyu Chu (1257-1302), Chao Mengfu (1254-1302)[3], and Yu Shihnan (A.D. 558-638).

7. Paintings of Ma Yuan (during Southern Sung) and Shia Kuei (between 1195-1224).

---

[2] This order of preference is of course personal, with emphasis on calligraphy.

[3] 赵孟頫 (1254—1322)——编者注。

8. Paintings of Shen Shihtien (1427-1509) and Wen Chenming (1470-1559).

9. Cursive scripts of Chu Chihshan (1460-1526).

10. Correspondence of other famous writers.

11. Bronze vessels before Han and Tsin, with brilliant greens and reds.

12. Ancient jade.

13. Tang inkstones.

14. Famous, well-authenticated swords and *chin*.

15. Good Wutai and Sung editions of books.

16. Quaint rocks with rugged lines and beautiful form.

17. Old dwarf pines, fine rush grass sharp like needles, in a good basin.

18. Charming dark plums and bamboos.

19. Imported high quality incense.

20. Rare, beautiful foreign novelties.

21. Choice tea and good wine.

22. Delicacies of food from land and sea.

23. White porcelain and earthenware of an unduplicable color.

A scholar should know the relative value of things, like the order of the Founding Knights of the Tang Empire in the mind of the great founder. One should not follow the commercial dealers who place the highest value on the brittle porcelain of Shuanteh and Chenghua.[4]

When Meng Chang (A.D. 919-965) obtained a copy of the drawing of Chung Kuei [subduer of evil spirits] done by Wu Taotse (eighth century), he asked Huang Chuan [a famous painter] to make a change in it. Chung Kuei was gouging out the eye of a devil with the forefinger of his left hand, and Meng Chang wanted Huang to change it so that the thumb was doing it. Huang made a new drawing and presented it to him, saying, "When Wu made this drawing, the whole force of Chung Kuei's body was concentrated in the forefinger. I cannot change it [without changing the whole posture]. Your humble servant cannot hope to equal Wu. But the whole force of this painting of mine is also concentrated, on the tip of the

---

[4] These were comparatively recent in the author's time.

thumb." I often tell this story to people who come to me with a piece and composition and beg me to correct it, and make them understand why I decline.

Calligraphy[5]

We must learn calligraphy as young men learn boxing or wrestling. Everybody knows how to close a fist or to stand firm. What one must learn is the posture for springing into action. If the posture is right, the wrestler can spring and leap and have the opponent in his mortal grip. The onlookers see all the rhythmic movements, the writhing and tugging and well-timed punching.

---

[5] The esthetics of calligraphy is based on the beauty of movement, not of static proportions. The nearest analogy is to call it dancing on paper, with its pauses, twirls, and well-timed stately steps. What makes it difficult is that it cannot be corrected. Each character written is evidence of a complicated involuting movement of the brush, and the pleasure consists in following that movement. The same beauty of mastery may be seen in the drives and cuts and chops on the tennis court as played by a champion. On the very sensitive, specially prepared paper, every slightest nuance or hesitation in the movement is recorded as on a photographic plate.

In writing characters, one must keep the spirits calm and feel suffused with an air of well-being, which he directs to the tip of his writing brush. Thus the writing flows out like a gentle breeze, or dots like sweet rain, or lashes down like a cataract, or pauses and is poised like curling and twisting angry pines. It goes fast or slow, as the situation demands, sweeps out or cuts in, never a step transgressing the way of the ancient models. The mind becomes the master, doing what it likes. In this way, one can hope to gain a little place among the calligraphists.

Matteo Ricci

[After discussing the people of Europe and their astronomy, the author continues.] In the last years of the previous reign, Matteo Ricci came out with ten associates, sailed 60,000 *li* [20,000 miles!], passing through more than a thousand countries, and reached Indo-China after six years. By the time he had reached the Kwangtung province [in which lies Canton], his fellow travelers had all died. Matteo had magic which protected him from all harm and he understood controlled breathing and internal vision [yoga], so he was free from sickness. He stopped at Kwangtung for over twenty years and understood the Chinese language and writing. He had a reddish beard and blue eyes and a rosy complexion. He was very polite, bowing when he met people, and people loved him, believing that he was a good man. I met him in the fall of 1597 at Kiukiang, and had a good talk with him. He showed me some strange things from his country, a painted glass screen, and a sand filter shaped like a goose egg. It is filled with sand which falls down to the lower end and can be reversed, and is used for keeping time. He had with him the sacred books of his country, which were ornamented with gold and precious stones. Its paper was smooth like a lady's flesh—I do not know what it is made of. He said that this was made from barks in his country and made thin like that. He was already over fifty and looked like one between twenty and thirty, being a distant tribesman who has learned the truth [in the Taoist sense]. He has roamed the world and come this far, and is not thinking of going home.

Money and Women

There are two things in this life which most quickly dissipate a man's energy and shorten his life—money and women. Magicians say that they can transmute base metal into gold to help people and that by practicing the art of love one can prolong life. Thus one can both get a great deal of pleasure and receive benefits. It is a very tempting proposition. But I do not believe it. I think it is too good to be true.[6]

---

[6] The art of "riding women" for health and long life, of "absorbing *yin* to strengthen *yang*," is at least as old as the time of Han Wuti (second century B.C.). The *Hanwu Kushih* of Pan Ku tells of many Taoists who by practicing this art lived to a great old age, without their hair turning white. The Emperor Han Wuti encouraged such magicians in his search for the magic formula of prolonging life, and he himself never slept without women. The legend was that he was a kind of maniac, and after his official burial in a mausoleum, when the palace girls were sent off to a monastery his ghost came to visit them, but other people could not see it. The number of women was therefore increased to five hundred to please him, and then the ghost disappeared.

【 紫桃轩杂缀（节录）】

明·李日华

　　陈郡丞尝为余言："黄子久终日只在荒山、乱石、丛木、深篠中坐，意态忽忽，人不测其为何。又每往泖中通海处，看激流轰浪，虽风雨骤至，水怪悲诧而不顾。"噫，此大痴之笔所以沉郁变化，几与造物争神奇哉！

　　昔顾恺之象人，张僧繇绘龙，俱不时点睛，以为神明在阿堵中也。山水林石家以苔为眉目，古人极不草草。尝闻白石翁积画一箧，俱未点苔，语人曰："今日意思昏钝，俟精明澄澈时为之耳。"

绘事要明取予。取者，形象仿佛处以笔勾取之，其致用虽在果毅，而妙运则贵玲珑断续；若直笔描画，即板结之病生矣。予者，笔断意含，如山之虚廓，树之去枝，凡有无之间是也。

山行，遇奇树怪石，即具楮墨，四面约略取之。此亦诗家李贺锦囊之储也。

作画如蒸云，度空触石，一任渺弥，遮露晦明，不可预定，要不失天成之致，乃为合作。学画如洗石，荡尽浮沙浊土，则灵窍自呈，秀色自现。二者于当境时卓竖真宰，于释用时深加观力，方有入路耳。

元·黄公望　富春山居图（局部）

今人不如古人，只是气魄雌下。所谓气魄，又不是咬牙弩睛所可强作者。然则何如？曰：于利害毁誉处，放教十分澹去，而一意与古人相求，自然不为世俗转换，而大妙可窥矣。

　　门人黄章甫索书，余因戏为评古次第云："晋、唐墨迹第一，五代、唐前、宋图画第二，隋、唐、宋古帖第三，苏、黄、蔡、米手迹第四，元人画第五，鲜于、虞、赵手迹第六，南宋马、夏绘事第七，国朝沈、文诸妙绘第八，祝京兆行草书第九，他名公杂札第十，

明·董其昌　高逸图

汉、秦以前彝鼎丹翠焕发者第十一，古玉珣璏之属第十二，唐砚第十三，古琴剑卓然名世者第十四，五代、宋精板书第十五，怪石嶙岣奇秀者第十六，老松苍瘦、蒲草细如针杪并得佳盆者第十七，梅竹诸卉清韵者第十八，舶香蕴藉者第十九，夷宝异丽者第二十，精茶法酝第二十一，山海异味第二十二，莹白妙磁、秘色陶器不论古今第二十三。外是则白饭、绿齑、布袍、藤杖亦为雅物。士人享用，当知次第，如汉凌烟阁中位次，明主自有灼见。若仅如俗贾，以宣成窑脆薄之品骤登上价，终是董贤作三公耳。

昔孟昶得吴道子画，钟馗左手第二指挖鬼睛。令黄筌改用拇指挖睛，筌乃别绷绢画以进曰："吴之画钟馗，一身力气意色，尽在第二指，不可改。臣画虽不迨吴，然一身力气意色，亦尽在拇指，不容移易。"竹懒曰："此作文法也。每有将他人所作文要余改窜，曰：'不敢深烦公，特备此朴以待斤斫也。'余辄出此一则辞之。"

吾辈学书，正如壮儿学手搏，岂是不能握拳筑脊，直是要学其势耳！得势则跳跃颠扑，动能制人死命，令旁观者见其雄逸震荡，以为天地且入其低昂簸弄中，奇态溢出矣。

写数字，必须萧散神情，吸取清和之气在于笔端，令挥则景风，洒则甘雨，引则飞泉直下，郁则怒松盘纠；乍疾乍徐，忽舒忽卷。按之无一笔不出古人，统之亹亹自行胸臆，斯为翰墨林中有少分相应处也。

至世庙末年，国人利玛窦者，结十伴航海漫游。历千余国，经六万里，凡六年抵安南，而入广东界。时从者俱死，玛窦有异术，人不能害。又善纳气内观，故疾瘵不作。居广二十余年，尽通中国语言文字。玛窦紫髯碧眼，面色如桃花。见人膜拜如礼，人亦爱之，信其为善人也。余丁酉秋，遇之豫章。与剧谈，出示国中异物，一玻璃画屏，一鹅卵沙漏，状如鹅卵，实沙其中，而颠倒渗泄之，以候更数。携有彼国经典，彩闟、金宝杂饰之。其纸如美妇之肌，不知何物也。云其国之树皮治薄之如此耳。玛窦年已五十余，如二三十岁人，盖远夷之得道者。汗漫至此，已不复作归计。

世间唯财与色能耗人精气，速人死亡。而方士之言曰："金银可点化以济世，少女可采药以长生。既快嗜欲，又得超胜，何惮而不为耶？"予以天理人情揆之，恐无此大便宜事，不敢信也。

On Zest in Life

Preface to *Hwheishin Collection of Poems of Chen Chengfu*

Yuan Chunglang

1568-1610

> Yuan Chunglang was leader of a literary school in the late
> Ming Dynasty known as the Kung-an School.

I find that zest is a rare gift in life. Zest is like hues on
the mountains, taste in water, brilliance in flowers, and
charm in women. It is appreciated only by those who have
understanding, and is difficult to explain in words. True
enough, it is common nowadays to find people who affect a
taste in certain diversions. Some cultivate a love for painting,
calligraphy, and antiques, and others are fascinated by the
mystics and the recluses and the life of a hermit. Still others
are like the people of Soochow who make a hobby of tea and

incense, turning it almost into a cult. These are superficial, and have nothing to do with real zest and understanding of the flavor in living.

This zest for living is more born in us than cultivated. Children have most of it. They have probably never heard of the word "zest," but they show it everywhere. They find it hard to look solemn; they wink, they grimace, they mumble to themselves, they jump and skip and hop and romp. That is why childhood is the happiest period of a man's life, and why Mencius spoke of "recovering the heart of a child" and Laotse referred to it as a model of man's original nature. The peasants who live near the mountains and forests do not make a cult of these things; in their life of freedom and absence of social conventions, they enjoy the beauties of nature all as a part of their living. The more degenerate men become, the harder they find it to enjoy life. Some are fascinated by merely sensual enjoyments and call it "fun," and find their pleasure in meats and wines and sex and riotous living and defiance of social customs, saying they are thus liberating themselves. Often as one progresses in life, his official rank becomes higher and his social status grows bigger; his body and mind are fettered with a thousand cares and sober duties. Then knowledge, learning, and life experience stop up even his pores and seep down to his hardened joints. The more he knows, the more befuddled he becomes, and the more removed he is from understanding this zest in living.

【 叙陈正甫会心集 】

明·袁宏道

　　世人所难得者唯趣。趣如山上之色，水中之味，花中之光，女中之态，虽善说者不能一语，唯会心者知之。今之人，慕趣之名，求趣之似，于是有辨说书画，涉猎古董，以为清；寄意玄虚，脱迹尘纷，以为远。又其下，则有如苏州之烧香煮茶者。此等皆趣之皮毛，何关神情！夫趣得之自然者深，得之学问者浅。当其为童子也，不知有趣，然无往而非趣也。面无端容，目无定睛；口喃喃而欲语，足跳跃而不定；人生之至乐，真无逾于此时者。孟子所谓不失赤子，老子所谓能婴儿，盖指此也，趣之正等正觉最上乘也。山林之人，无拘无缚，得自在度日，故虽不求趣而趣近之。愚不肖之近趣也，以无品也。品愈卑，故所求愈下。或为酒肉，或然声伎；率心而行，无所忌惮，自以为绝望于世，故举世非笑之不顾也，此又一趣也。迨夫年渐长，官渐高，品渐大，有身如梏，有心如棘，毛孔骨节，俱为闻见知识所缚，入理愈深，然其去趣愈远矣。余友陈正甫，深于趣者也，故所述《会心集》若干人，趣居其多。不然，虽介若伯夷，高若严光，不录也。噫！孰谓有品如君，官如君，年之壮如君，而能知趣如此者哉！

明·仇英　蕉荫结夏图（局部）

Lovers of Flowers

Yuan Chunglang

1568-1610

I have found that all the people in the world who are dull in their
conversation and hateful to look at in their faces are those who
have no hobbies.... When the ancient people who had a weakness
for flowers heard there was a remarkable variety, they would
travel across high mountain passes and deep ravines in search of
them, unconscious of bodily fatigue, bitter cold or scorching heat,
and their peeling skins, and completely oblivious of their bodies
soiled with mud. When a flower was about to bud, they would
move their beds and pillows to sleep under them, watching how
the flowers passed from infancy to maturity and finally dropped
off and died. Or they would plant thousands in their orchards
to study how they varied, or have just a few in their rooms to
exhaust their interest. Some would be able to tell the size of
flowers from smelling their leaves, and some were able to tell from
the roots the color of their flowers. These were the people who
were true lovers of flowers and who had a true weakness for them.

【 好事 】

明·袁宏道

稽康之锻也，武子之马也，陆羽之茶也，米颠之石也，倪云林之洁也，皆以癖而寄其磊块俊逸之气者也。余观世上语言无味、面目可憎之人，皆无癖之人耳。若真有所癖，将沉湎酣溺，性命死生以之，何暇及钱奴宦贾之事？古之负花癖者，闻人谈一异花，虽深谷峻岭，不惮蹒跚而从之，至于浓寒盛暑，皮肤皴鳞，汗垢如泥，皆所不知。一花将萼，则移枕携褥，睡卧其下，以观花之由微至盛至落至于萎地而后去。或千株万本以穷其变，或单枝数房以极其趣，或嗅叶而知花之大小，或见根而辨色之红白。是之谓真爱

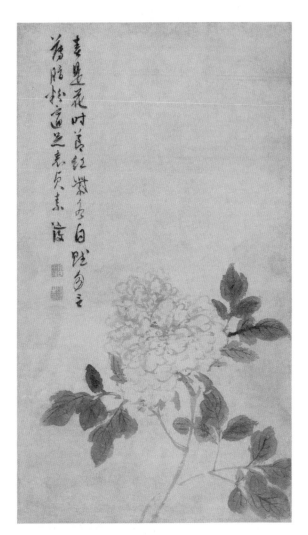

春來花时节红紫斗芳菲自怜闲地……
若肠将遂之素贞秉贞 复

明·陈道复　牡丹花卉图

花，是之谓真好事也。若夫石公之养花，聊以破闲居

孤寂之苦，非真能好之也。夫使其真好之，已为桃花

洞口人矣，尚复为人间尘土之官哉？

In Memory of a Child

"Sacrificial Prayer to Ah Chen"

Shen Chunlieh

?-1624

> I think this is one of the most tender things I ever read,
> especially toward the end.

On the twenty-third of December of the year 1619, Shen
Chunlieh's eldest daughter, Ah Chen, died of smallpox which
failed to appear, and was buried on the northern mounds. Her
mother, Madame Po, recited Buddhist sutras daily in her favor,
and urged the writing of a sacrificial prayer for her, but he did
not have the heart to take up a pen and do it. On the twenty-
first day of her death, he prepared for her a sacrifice of cooked
food, and composed a piece to weep over her, which was burned
on the scene of her childhood games, and is as follows:

Alas! great is my sorrow! Your name is Ah Chen, written with the components Ping and Chen, because you were born in the year Pingchen (1616). When you were born, I was not truly pleased, for I was a man over thirty, and you came not a boy but a girl. But before you were one year old, you were already adorable. When one nodded to you, you opened your mouth and laughed. During this period, Chouma [amah] was taking care of you, and she woke up ten times a night, and never took off her girdle while going to bed. When you were hungry, you sought for milk from your mama, and when you were well filled, you went to bed with Chouma. And Chouma suffered many misunderstandings on your account. She moved you from a wet place to a dry place, and went to great troubles to lighten a small suffering. If she paid you too much attention, your mother would reprimand her, and if she paid too little attention, you would cry.

Last year, I was unlucky. On account of the examinations, I had to tear myself away from you. I failed in the examinations and

Chouma died. When I came back, you pulled at my sleeves and asked for toys. With you by my side, my sorrow was relieved. You grew more teeth and you daily grew in wisdom. You called "Dada" and "Mama" and your pronunciation was perfect. You often knocked at the door and asked "Who is it?" When my nephew came, you called him "Koko" [elder brother]. He took away your toys in play and you ran away and protested. When your maternal uncle came, you pulled at his gown. You called out "Mama" and you laughed in a silvery voice. When your paternal uncle came, you played the host. Lifting the cup, you said, "Ching!" and we roared with laughter. Your grandpa went to the country, and you yourself went to Soochow. For a year you had not seen him, and we asked you if you knew grandpa, and you said, "Yes. White cap and white beard." You had never seen your maternal grandpa, and when we asked you, "Whence comes this guest?" you said "Peking!" Your maternal grandma was very fond of you and regarded you like her own. Several times she took you to Soochow with her. You asked for toys at midnight and asked for fruit at day's dawn. Your own parents asked you to come home, but you refused, saying "Grandma would think of me."

This year in June, you had boils, and I went to Soochow specially to take you home. I touched your affected spots, and your face showed pain. But you did not cry, thinking it was not right. Every time you took a fruit or sweetmeat, you looked at people's faces, and if we did not approve, you would not put it in your mouth. Sometimes you touched things and accidentally spoiled them, and one just looked at you, and your hand would shrink back. Your mama was too strict with you, and she often admonished you, for fear that when you grew up, you would form such habits. I did not agree, and told her in private, "Let the baby alone. What does she know at this young age?" When you were at Soochow, and mama and I were coming home, we asked you if you would come or stay. And your heart lay both ways, and you hesitated to reply. Then you came home, and we were so glad, and we coaxed you and we pulled faces to get your laugh. You carried a toy basket of dates and sat on a low stool to eat porridge. You repeated the "Great Learning," and you bowed to Buddha. You played at guessing games, and you romped about the house. You clapped your hands and thought yourself very clever.

But within a fortnight, the day of your death came. Was it Heaven's will or was it your fate? Even the fairies do not know. Before you died, we sent for a doctor. Some said it was a cold, and some said it was smallpox. It could not be a cold, and it might be smallpox, and we still wonder what you died of. You were clever at speech, but you were silent then. You only panted and stared at us. We wept around you and you wept, too.

Alas! great is my sorrow! According to conventions, why should one weep at a daughter's death. According to my age, I am in my prime and poor and alone. You were very intelligent, and I was satisfied with you, although a girl. But who knew that the gods would be so cruel to me? Ten days before you, your younger sister, Ah Shun, died of the same disease in three days.

You know her well, and now that you have no company there, you must stick together with your sister. You can already walk about, but your sister can hardly stand steadily. You should take her by the hand and go about together and must be good to each other and never quarrel. If you meet your amah [Chouma], you could ask her, saying, "Pa had a wife by the name of Ku and a mammy by the name of Min." Ask her to take you to them, and they will surely take care of you. You can stay there for the present, and you should be near Ku. Sister is small and you should lead her, and you are small and Ku should protect you. Sometime later, I will find a propitious ground and bury you three in the same grave.

I am thinking of you now, and it is hard to forget you. If you should hear my prayer, come to see me in my dreams. If fate decrees that you must yet live an earthly life, then come again into your mama's womb. I am offering Buddhist sacrifices and prayers, and I have soup here for you, and I am burning paper money for your use. When you see the Judge of the Lower

World, hold your hands together and plead to him, "I am young, and I am innocent. I was born in a poor family and I was contented with scanty meals. I never wasted a single grain of rice, and I was never willfully careless of my clothing and my shoes. Whatever thou commandest, I am only a young child. If evil spirits ever bully me, may thou protect me!" You should just put it that way, and you should not cry or make too much noise. For remember you are in a strange underworld, and it is not like it is at home with our own people. Now I am composing this, but you do not yet know how to read. I will only cry, "Ah Chen, your father is here." I can but cry for you and call your name.

【 祭震女文 】

明·沈君烈

万历己未年冬下浣之三日，沈承之长女阿震以痘不发而殇，藁葬北邙之次。其母薄氏，日称念梵书，资其冥福，复促作一疏词，笔不忍下也。于其三七，当荐熟食，乃为文哭之，焚其所生前跳弄之场，曰：呜呼痛哉！汝名阿震，生于丙辰。以丙辰字，故取震名。汝生之初，我实不喜，三十许人，不男而女。追汝未期，汝即可怜，以颔招汝，汝笑哑然。当此之时，周妪褓汝，衣不解带，一夜十起。饱就妪眠，饥就母乳，妪因汝故，亦几委曲。移湿就干，补疮剜肉，烦则母瞋，省则汝哭。昨岁戊午，我命不济，频出就试，割汝而去。周妪既死，试又不利，归来牵袖，索物而戏，有汝在侧，愁亦快意。汝齿日添，汝慧日多，呼爹呼姆，音不少讹。常手弹门，自问谁何？我侄来时，汝呼曰哥，戏攫汝物，汝窜而波。我舅来时，汝以衣拖，呼声曰母，旋笑呵呵。汝伯来时，作宾主陪，擎杯曰请，笑者如雷。汝祖入乡，汝又往苏，经年不值，问汝识无，应声曰识，白帽白须。汝有外翁，一面未曾，问客何方？即曰北京。汝之外姑，视如身生，凡三五次，挈汝苏行。三更索玩，五更索果，父母留汝，汝反不可。顾谓我曰：阿婆思我。今年六月，汝有疖灾，我特往苏，挈汝归来。摩沙患处，其色甚哀，然不敢哭，恐哭不该。每持果饵，必窥意旨，不色授之，不遽入齿。每手玩弄，误有损伤，小目怒之，敛手退藏。汝母过严，时加梏束，惧汝长大，习惯成熟。我意亦然，但私相嘱，婴孩何知，且随其欲。汝昔在苏，父母归娄，问汝何依，欲去欲留？言虽不决，意在两头。顷汝归斯，喜不自持，诱汝怖汝，假面作痴，小筐提枣，矮座啜糜。口诵《大学》，手拜阿弥。握枚赌胜，绕屋争驰。哈哈拍掌，自喜为奇。不勾半月，即汝死期，天乎命乎，神仙莫知。汝未死顷，召医诊视，或云风邪，或云癫子。风不可必，癫似有理，至今思之，不测所以。汝善话言，此际不语，声嘶气断，张目而已。环汝而泣，汝泪亦泚。呜呼！痛可忍言哉！论世俗情，女死何哭？论我生年，壮大穷独，汝又颇慧，虽女亦足，谁知鬼神，虐我太酷。先汝十日，

沐堂仁兄先生雅属即求
教之壬午五月朔山阴
任颐伯年写

写于春申浦上寓斋

清·任颐　仕女婴戏图

汝妹阿巽，少汝二岁，与汝同病，同三日亡，汝所狎认，今汝无伴，当与妹并。汝稍能行，妹立未定，往来携手，相好无竞。若逢汝妪，可更一问，父有室顾，父有姒闵。但往依之，必汝提引，所以权厝，亦近顾侧。妹小汝携，汝小顾披，他年卜地，葬汝同宅。我今思汝，不能去怀，汝若有知，常入梦来。缘或未尽，可再投胎。所谓金刚，并诸经咒，设羹燔钱，付汝领受。汝见冥王，操手哀叩：侬实不寿，侬实无咎。侬生贫家，侬甘粗陋，糁粒必拾，以畏雷吼。襦履必惜，以爬微垢。神有诛求，侬年实幼。鬼有陵轹，望神为佑。但可如是，莫啼莫哗，地府之中，不比在家。我今作文，汝不识字，但呼阿震，汝父在此。哭汝一声，呼汝一次。

Harvest Moon on West Lake

From *Dream Memories of West Lake*

Chang Tai

1597-1689

> The author was born in a family of high officials, enjoying
> fabulous luxury. After the Ming Dynasty fell, he lived in
> reduced circumstances but persisted in his life as author
> with proud independence. Some of his most charming
> writings are his recollections of the West Lake of
> Hangchow. He always writes in a highly individualistic,
> pithy style.

There is nothing to see during the harvest moon on West
Lake [Hangchow]. All you can see are people who come out
to see the moon. Briefly, there are five categories of these
holidaymakers. First, there are those who come out in the
name of looking at the harvest moon, but never even take
a look at it: the people who, expensively dressed, sit down

at gorgeous dinners with music in brightly illuminated boats or villas, in a confusion of light and noise. Secondly, those who do sit in the moonlight, but never look at it: ladies, daughters of high families, in boats and towers, also handsome boys [homosexuals] who sit in open spaces and giggle and chatter and look at other people. Thirdly, boat parties of famous courtesans and monks with time on their hands who enjoy a little sip and indulge in song and flute and string instruments. They are in the moonlight, too, and indeed look at the moon, but want people to see them looking at the moon. Fourthly, there are the young men, who neither ride, nor go into boats, but after a drink and a good dinner, rush about in their rowdy dress and seek the crowd at Chaoching and Tuanchiao where it is thickest, shouting, singing songs of no known melody, and pretending to be drunk. They look at the moon, look at the people looking at the moon, and also look at those not looking at the moon, but actually see nothing. Lastly, there are those who hire a small boat, provided with a clay stove and a clean table and

choice porcelain cups and pots, and who get into the boat
with a few friends and their sweethearts; they hide under a
tree or row out into the Inner Lake in order to escape from
the crowd, and look at the moon without letting people
see that they are looking at the moon and even without
consciously looking at it.

The local Hangchow people come out on the lake, if they
do at all, between eleven in the morning and eight in the
evening, as if they had a morbid fear of the moon. But on
this night, they all come out in groups, in the hope of getting
good tips. The sedan chair carriers line up on the bank. The
moment they get into a boat, they tell the boatman to hurry
and row across to the Tuanchiao area, and get lost in the
crowd. Therefore in that area before the second watch [ten
o'clock], the place is filled with noise and music bands in a
weird, boiling confusion, like a roaring sea or a landslide, or
a nightmare, or like Bedlam let loose, with all the people in
it rendered deaf for the moment. Large and small boats are

tied up along the bank, and one can see nothing except boats creaking against boats, punting poles knocking punting poles, shoulders rubbing shoulders, and faces looking at faces. Soon the feasting is over, the officials leave, the yamen runners shout to clear the way, the sedan chair carriers scream for fare, the boatmen give warning that the city gates will soon be closed. A grand procession of torches and lanterns, with swarms of retainers, passes on. Those on land also hurry to get into the city before the closing of the gate, and very soon almost the entire crowd is gone.

Only then do we move the boat to Tuanchiao. The rocks have become cool by this time, and we spread a mat on the ground and invite ourselves to a great drink. At this time, the moon looks like a newly polished mirror, the hills appear draped in a new dress, and the face of the lake is like a lady after a fresh make-up. Those who have been hiding themselves under a tree and enjoying a quiet sip come out now also. We exchange names and invite them to join us.

There we have charming friends and famous courtesans; cups and chopsticks are in place, and songs and music begin, in the chilly dream world of moonlight. The party breaks up at dawn, and we get into the boat again and move it into the miles of lotus-covered surface, where we catch a nap in an air filled with its fragrance, and have a perfect sleep.

【 西湖七月半 】

明·张岱

西湖七月半，一无可看，止可看看七月半之人。看七月半之人，以五类看之。其一，楼船箫鼓，峨冠盛筵，灯火优傒，声光相乱，名为看月而实不见月者，看之；其一，亦船亦楼，名娃闺秀，携及童娈，笑啼杂之，还坐露台，左右盼望，身在月下而实不看月者，看之；其一，亦船亦声歌，名妓闲僧，浅斟低唱，弱管轻丝，竹肉相发，亦在月下，亦看月而欲人看其看月者，看之；其一，不舟不车，不衫不帻，酒醉饭饱，呼群三五，跻入人丛，昭庆、断桥，嘄呼嘈杂，装假醉，唱无腔曲，月亦看，看月者亦看，不看月者亦看，而实无一看者，看之；其一，小船轻幌，净几暖炉，茶铛旋煮，素瓷静递，好友佳人，邀月同坐，或匿影树下，或逃嚣里湖，看月而人不见其看月之态，亦不作意看者，看之。

杭人游湖，巳出酉归，避月如仇。是夕好名，逐队争出，多犒门军酒钱，轿夫擎燎，列俟岸上。一入舟，速舟子急放断桥，赶入胜会。以故二鼓以前人声鼓吹，如沸如撼，如魇如呓，如聋如哑。大船小船一齐凑岸，一无所见，止见篙击篙，舟触舟，肩摩肩，脸看脸而已。少刻兴尽，官府席散，皂隶喝道去，轿夫叫船上人，怖以关门，灯笼火把如列星，一一簇拥而去。岸上人亦逐队赶门，渐稀渐薄，顷刻散尽矣。

明·李流芳　西湖烟雨图（局部）

　　吾辈始舣舟近岸。断桥石磴始凉，席其上，呼

客纵饮。此时月如镜新磨，山复整妆，湖复颒面，向

之浅斟低唱者出，匿影树下者亦出，吾辈往通声气，

拉与同坐。韵友来，名妓至，杯箸安，竹肉发。月色苍凉，东方将白，客方散去。吾辈纵舟，酣睡于十里荷花之中，香气拍人，清梦甚惬。

Professional Matchmakers

From *Dream Memories of West Lake*

Chang Tai

1597-1689

> The original title is "Lean Horses," local name for
> matchmakers. The author describes the practice of
> Yangchow, nationally famed as the center of luxury and
> the place where regular houses trained girls to be singsong
> artists or concubines. The time was the early seventeenth
> century.

> This piece describes what may be called the "concubine
> market" and its efficiency. It is the most unromantic way of
> securing a mistress; only coarse businessmen would buy a
> concubine this way.

At Yangchow, there were hundreds of people making a
living from activities connected with the "lean horses." One
should never let it be known that one was looking for a

concubine. Once this leaked out, the professional agents and go-betweens, both men and women, would swarm about his house or hotel like flies, and there was no way of keeping them off. The next morning, he would find many of them waiting for him, and the matchmaker who arrived first would hustle him off, while the rest followed behind and waited for their chance.

Arriving at the house of the "lean horse," the person would be served tea as soon as he was seated. At once the woman agent would come out with a girl and announce, "*Kuniang*" [mademoiselle], curtsy!" The girl curtsied. Next was said, "*Kuniang*, walk forward!" She walked forward. "*Kuniang*, turn around!" She turned around, facing the light, and her face was shown. "Pardon, can we have a look at your hand?" The woman rolled up her sleeve and exposed her entire arm. Her skin was shown. "*Kuniang*, look at the gentleman." She looked from the corner of her eyes. Her eyes were shown. "How old is *Kuniang*?"

She replied. Her voice was shown. "Please walk again a bit."
This time the woman lifted her skirts. Her feet were shown.
There is a secret about judging women's feet. When you hear
the rustle of her skirts when she comes out, you may guess that
she has big feet, but if she wears her skirts relatively high and
reveals her feet as she takes a step forward, you already know
that she has a pair of small feet that she is proud of. "*Kuniang*,
you can go back."

As soon as the girl went in, another came out and the same
thing was repeated. Usually there were five or six girls in a
house. If the gentleman decided he would take a certain girl,
he would put a gold hairpin or ornament on her hair; this was
called *tsatai*. If no one was satisfactory, a tip of several hundred
cash was given the woman agent or the maids of the house, and
one was shown another house. When one woman agent had
completed the round of the houses she operated with, other
women agents came around. Thus it continued for one, two,

perhaps four or five days. There was no end to it and the agents were never tired. But after one had seen fifty or sixty of them, they were all just about alike, with a painted face and a red dress. It is like writing characters; by the time you have made the same sign a hundred times or a thousand times, you cannot recognize it any more. One does not know what to decide or which one to take, and eventually makes his choice on one of them.

After the choice was made, signaled by *tsatai*, the owner came out with a red sheet of paper and a writing brush. On the paper were written the items: silks, gold flowers, cash present, and pieces of cloth. The owner would dip the brush in ink and hold it ready for the customer to fill in the number of pieces and the cash present he was prepared to give for the girl. If this was satisfactory, the deal was concluded and the customer took his leave.

Before he arrived at his own place, drummers and musicians and carrier-loads of lamb and red and green wines were already there. In a moment, ceremonial papers, fruit, and pastry also arrived, and the senders went back accompanied by the musicians. Before they had gone a quarter mile, there came back with the band, floral sedan chairs, floral lanterns, torches, handled torches, sedan chair carriers, bridesmaids, candles, more fruit, and roasts. The cook arrived with a carrier-load of vegetables and meats, sweets, followed by awnings, tablecloths, chair cushions, table service, longevity stars, bed curtains, and string instruments. Without notice and even without asking for approval, the floral sedan chair and another chair supposed to accompany the bride started off to welcome the bride with a procession of bridal lanterns and handled torches. Before you knew it, the bride had arrived. The bride camp up and performed the wedding ceremony [by bowing to the groom and guests], and she was ushered to take her place at the dinner table already laid.

Music and song began, and there was much ado about the house. Everything was efficient and fast. Before noon, the agent asked for her tip, said good-by, and rushed off to look for other customers.

【 扬州瘦马 】

明·张岱

　　扬州人日饮食于瘦马之身者数十百人。娶妾者切勿露意，稍透消息，牙婆驵侩，咸集其门，如蝇附膻，撩扑不去。黎明，即促之出门，媒人先到者先挟之去，其余尾其后，接踵伺之。至瘦马家，坐定，进茶，牙婆扶瘦马出，曰："姑娘拜客。"下拜。曰："姑娘往上走。"走。曰："姑娘转身。"转身向明立，面出。曰："姑娘借手睄睄。"尽褫其袂，手出，臂出，肤亦出。曰："姑娘睄相公。"转眼偷觑，眼出。曰："姑娘几岁？"曰几岁，声出。曰："姑娘再走走。"以手拉其裙，趾出。然看趾有法，凡出门裙幅先响者，

152

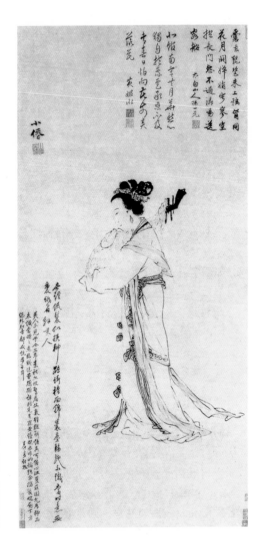

明·吴伟　琵琶美人图

必大；高系其裙，人未出而趾先出者，必小。曰："姑娘请回。"一人进，一人又出。看一家必五六人，咸如之。看中者，用金簪或钗一股插其鬓，曰"插带"。看不中，出钱数百文，赏牙婆或赏其家侍婢，又去看。牙婆倦，又有数牙婆踵伺之。一日、二日至四五日，不倦亦不尽，然看至五六十人，白面红衫，千篇一律，如学字者，一字写至百至千，连此字亦不认得矣。心与目谋，毫无把柄，不得不聊且迁就，定其一人。

"插带"后，本家出一红单，上写彩缎若干，金花若干，财礼若干，布匹若干，用笔蘸墨，送客点阅。客批财礼及缎匹如其意，则肃客归。归未抵寓，而鼓乐盘担、红绿羊酒在其门久矣。不一刻，而礼币、糕果俱齐，鼓乐导之去。去未半里，而花轿花灯、擎燎火把、山人傧相、纸烛供果牲醴之属，门前环侍。厨子挑一担至，则蔬果、肴馔、汤点、花棚、糖饼、桌围坐褥、酒壶杯箸、龙虎寿星、撒帐牵红、小唱弦索之类，又毕备矣。不待复命，亦不待主人命，而花轿及亲送小轿一齐往迎，鼓乐灯燎，新人轿与亲送轿一时俱到矣。新人拜堂，亲送上席，小唱鼓吹，喧阗热闹。日未午而讨赏遽去，急往他家，又复如是。

The Discovery of Self

Preface to *Selected Poems of Langhuan*

Chang Tai

1597-1689

> The literary schools mentioned here which the author
> tried in his younger days to imitate, are known generally
> as (1) the Kung-an School of the three Yuan brothers, led
> by Yuan Chunglang, flourishing around the year 1600,
> and (2) the Chingling School, a reaction against the first,
> led by Chung Poching (died 1625) and Tan Yuanchun
> (died 1631). The Kung-an School emphasized the
> expression of a writer's personality and a style of natural
> simplicity, sometimes carried to the point of bareness. The
> other school went in for a style packed with the intricate,
> the abstruse and difficult. Shu Wenchang, the idol of the
> author and of Yuan Chunglang, was an eccentric genius,
> poet, and playwright who lived from 1521 to 1593. The
> style here is deliberately quaint.

In my young days, I loved [Shu] Wenchang, and began to learn

writing verse in his style. Because [Yuan] Chunglang liked

Wenchang also, I also began to learn to write like Chunglang who liked Wenchang. I never tried to write like others before these two. Later I liked the Chingling School and thought of writing like Tan and Chung, but never really had the time to master it. My friend Chang Yiju liked the latter school. He made an anthology of poetry from the Chung and Tan point of view, and from the same point of view selected my poems which tried to be like Chung and Tan but could never equal them. He said my poems very much resembled Wenchang in spirit, and he left these alone and selected only those which more or less caught the Chung-Tan spirit. I decided to reform, and burnt all those poems which suggested resemblance to Wenchang, and tortured my brains to write nothing except that which was in the Chung-Tan tradition.

After ten years, I examined myself and found that I had failed to learn the style of Chung and Tan. For my nature was born like Wenchang. I might change a few words to give the verse a different complexion, but my bones could not be changed.

I began to realize that the writing of a man is like the form and shape and petals and arrangement of flowers. These grow spontaneously in accordance with their inner nature, and take certain forms without mistake and without fail. One can graft another variety, and although certain changes may be produced, the main structural forms cannot be changed. I had already burnt those poems à la Wenchang. Now if I burned also those poems seemingly à la Chung and Tan, but essentially à la Wenchang, I would have to burn everything I ever wrote. I decided to spare these in time, and had copies made for my children, so that they would know that once their father was also a poet, that he both learned poems à la Wenchang and burned poems à la Wenchang, and but had now decided to preserve some which resemble Wenchang. These I preserve so that part of Tsungtse (myself) which resembles Wenchang may be preserved, and the Wenchang which is copied by Tsungtse may also be preserved through me. So if Tsungtse and Wenchang are both preserved, then the Wenchang spirit in Wenchang poems burned by Yiju will also be preserved.

My old friend Wu Shi used to say that I am a reincarnation of Wenchang. He came especially to collect his poems and my discarded poems. But the poems of mine which he published are not equal to the poems of Wenchang which were published before. This means that already in his previous life Wenchang was not as good as Wenchang.

Now if one is going to take that Wenchang which was not as good as Wenchang and try to put into a pigeonhole the Tsungtse which resembles Wenchang without trying, Tsungtse will not submit to such treatment. The ancients said well, "I will try to get along with my own self." So I must learn to express myself.

The fifteenth of August, 1654.

【《琅嬛诗集》序】

明·张岱

余少喜文长，遂学文长诗。因中郎喜文长，而并学喜文长之中郎诗，文长、中郎以前无学也。后喜钟、谭诗，复欲学钟、谭诗，而鹿鹿无暇，伯敬、友夏，虽好之而未及学也。张毅儒，好钟、谭者也，以钟、谭手眼选明诗，遂以钟、谭手眼选余之好钟、谭而不及学钟、谭之明诗，其去取故有在也。毅儒言予诗酷似文长，以其似文长者姑置之，而选及余之稍似钟、谭者。予乃始知自悔，举向所为似文长者悉烧之，而涤骨刮肠，非钟、谭则一字不敢置笔。刻苦十年，乃问所为学钟、谭者又复不似。盖语出胞胎，即略有改移，亦不过头面，而求其骨格，则仍一文长也。余于是知人之诗文，如天生草木花卉，其色之红黄，瓣之疏密，如印板一一印出，无纤毫稍错。世人即以他木接之，虽形状少异，其大致不能尽改也。

余既取其似文长者而烧之矣，今又取其稍似钟、谭而终似文长者又烧之，则余诗无不当烧者矣。余今乃大悟，简余所欲烧而不及烧者悉存之，得若干首，抄付儿辈，使儿辈知其父少年亦曾学诗，亦曾学文长之诗，亦曾烧诗之似文长者，而今又复存其似文长之诗。存其似者，则存其似文长之宗子；存其似之者，则并存其宗子所似之文长矣。宗子存而文长不得存，宗子文长存而烧文长，文长之毅儒，亦不得不存矣。

向年余老友吴系曾梦文长说余是其后身，此来专为收其佚稿。及予选佚稿，而其所刻诸诗，实不及文长以前所刻之诗，则是文长生前已遂不及文长矣。今日举不及文长之文长，乃欲以笼络不必学文长而似文长之宗子，则宗子肯复受哉。古人曰："我与我周旋久，则宁学我。"

甲午八月望日，陶庵老人张岱书于快园之渴旦庐。

老夫遊戲墨淋漓，
花草都將雜四時，
莫怪畫圖差兩筆，
近來天道較差池。

觀黥山儂

明·徐渭　四季花卉图

163

The Half-and-Half Song

Li Mi-an

16th century?

> This is the soundest and most mature philosophy of living
> comprised in a single poem that I know, although I know,
> too, that it is one of the most exasperating to the hundred-
> percenters.

By far the greater half have I seen through

This floating life—ah, there's the magic word—

This "half"—so rich in implications.

It bids us taste the joy of more than we

Can ever own. Halfway in life is man's

Best state, when slackened pace allows him ease.

A wide world lies halfway 'twixt heaven and earth;

To live halfway between the town and land,

Have farms halfway between the streams and hills;

Be half-a-scholar, and half-a-squire, and half

In business; half as gentry live,

And half related to the common folk;

And have a house that's half genteel, half plain,

Half elegantly furnished and half bare;

Dresses and gowns that are half old, half new,

And food half epicure's, half simple fare;

Have servants not too clever, nor too dull;

A wife who is not too ugly, nor too fair.

—So then, at heart, I feel I'm half a Buddha,

And almost half a Taoist fairy blest.

One half myself to Father Heaven I

Return; the other half to children leave—

Half thinking how for my posterity

To plan and provide, and yet minding how

To answer God when the body's laid at rest.

He is most wisely drunk who is half drunk;
And flowers in half-bloom look their prettiest;
As boats at half-sail sail the steadiest,
And horses held at half-slack reins trot best.

Who half too much has, adds anxiety,
But half too little, adds possession's zest.
Since life's of sweet and bitter compounded,
Who tastes but half is wise and cleverest.

【 半半歌 】

清·李密庵

看破浮生过半，半之受用无边。

半中岁月尽幽闲，半里乾坤宽展。

半郭半乡村舍，半山半水田园，

半耕半读半经廛，半士半姻民眷。

半雅半粗器具，半华半实庭轩，

衾裳半素半轻鲜，肴馔半丰半俭。

童仆半能半拙，妻儿半朴半贤，

心情半佛半神仙，姓字半藏半显。

一半还之天地，让将一半人间，

半思后代与沧田，半想阎罗怎见。

明·万邦治　醉饮图（局部）

饮酒半酣正好，花开半时偏妍，

半帆张扇免翻颠，马放半缰稳便。

半少却饶滋味，半多反厌纠缠，

百年苦乐半相参，会占便宜只半。

How to Relax

Chang Nai

c. 1600

> The Chinese title for this essay ("Shichishuo") means "The
> Mechanism of Rest." As in English, the word "to rest" is
> closely associated with "to refresh," "to restore," and "to
> recuperate," and further, even with the idea of growth. The
> Chinese word *shi* has all these meanings and, in addition,
> designates the "breath." This rest is regarded as a silent,
> continuous process, making for growth and restoration.

Since coming to the capital, I have occupied a room, where there
are two couches. Yu Shuho and I often sit and talk together,
or light an incense and read, and when we are tired, we lie
down, and after a while get up and read again. We rather enjoy
this kind of life. Sometimes, returning to our room, I used to
feel the place was too uncomfortably small, hardly conducive
to rest and relaxation. Then I realized with a smile that the

physical location should have nothing to do with it. Mencius spoke of the continuous process of "growth and recuperation" [*shi*] in trees and in men "day and night," and we speak of the expelling of breath in respiration as *shi*. We also speak of the growth and prosperity of plants and the multiplication of their kind in animals as *shengshi* and *tseshi*. It is clear then that this "rest" is associated with life, and not with death or cessation of activities. A good analogy is that of banking a furnace, or covering up a brazier with hot ashes; the fire goes on, ready to burst into flame when we add fuel to it. On the other hand, to mistake "rest" as a cessation of activities would be more like putting out the light in an oil lamp. This is the vulgar idea of sleep. When Mencius spoke of the "rest by day and night," he meant that the process of growth and restoring of balance was going on all the time. The breath is continually being inhaled and exhaled like the alternation of the sun and the moon, or like the ebb and flow of tides. It is a continuous process of repair and restoration of balance during activity, and not confined to the period of "rest" only. In this sense, a man who has trained

himself goes through his daily business and contacts with
people with possession of mind; he is never hustled when busy
and deals with the problems simply and clearly. Mr. Yangming[1]
kept on discussing philosophy even during his military
campaigns, which is a good example to prove that one can be
relaxed in time of busy activity. In plants, the flowers and fruit
grow above while the roots are hidden below, but there is not a
moment when waste is not being repaired and the plant is not
being nourished. A system of vital energy is circulating all the
time from its flowers and fruits to its roots, and when this flow
of vital energy is lacking or failing, there is neither growth nor
restoration.

Human life depends entirely upon this vital force. That is why
it is said that one must keep poise to maintain it. All thinking
and all deliberations come from this calm and poise, a state of

---

[1] Wang Yangming (1472-1528), a great philosopher of the Ming Dynasty who
taught the identity of knowledge and action ("acting is believing"). Note the
Chinese usage of addressing Mr. Wang as "Mr. Yangming," which is normal.
"Mr. Yangming" is polite; "Mr. Wang" is entirely impersonal.

complete rest from vexations when one can call oneself master of a situation. That is why it is also said, "Let the environment be disturbing, but let the mind be calm." For when the mind can master that equilibrium, one feels that the environmental circumstances cannot upset it. It is therefore not true that rest and relaxation depend upon one's physical location or circumstances.

The method is therefore not to seek relaxation in material conditions, but in the mind. One may well examine oneself: Am I calm or confused when there is a busy schedule morning and night? Do I sleep well? Do I talk too much, or give way too much to pride and anger? Am I dogmatic and self-opinionated, or am I detached, looking at life from the outside? If I can answer these questions in the affirmative, then I am continually being refreshed, and all activities go to nourish my vitality even as the fire in a banked brazier. If not, this vital force is dissipated and almost used up through hustling and bustling. In that case, even when sitting idly with one's eyes closed, one's mind is occupied with a booming confusion of thoughts, which is not a real rest. Man depends upon food to nourish his blood and keep up the balance between waste and repair. Some who are troubled spirits dream troubled dreams at night, or sit idly like a wooden corpse in the daytime. There are people today who try to do this, shutting themselves up in a quiet meditation hall and acting like a disemboweled spirit. Where is the trace of vitality and growth? A popular saying goes: "Tsang-men [the busy street of Soochow] is a good place for study," meaning that one can do it if one is master of oneself.

Shuho thinks that one should have a couch by the side of one's desk, where one can lie down when tired from meeting people, or reading or writing, or after various amusements or a long conversation. That will be achieving what may be called a "small [temporary] peace." Mr. Lungchi says, "A perfect man rests, but does not sleep." The breath of life restores, but in sleep a man's soul wanders away from his body. To seek this relaxation during the time of action and work would be achieving what may be called the "great [deep-down] peace." I write this for Shuho.

> An ancient saying says, "Flowing water does not stink,
> and a door hinge which is constantly used does not rot."
> Chuangtse says, "A perfect man does not dream," the
> notion of a perfect man being one with great spiritual
> powers. The quotation from Mencius referred to also makes
> the idea plain. Mencius says, "How can nature remain
> beautiful when it is hacked at every day as the woodsman
> chops down trees in a forest? To be sure, the nights and days
> do the healing and there is the nourishing air of the early
> dawn, but this is soon dissipated by what he does during
> the day. With this continuous hacking of the human spirit,
> the rest and recuperation obtained during the night are
> not sufficient to maintain its level, and when the night's
> recuperation and rest are not sufficient to maintain its level,
> the man degrades himself to a state not far from that of a
> beast. People see that he acts like a beast and imagine that
> there was never any true character in him. But is this the
> true nature of man?"

【 息机说 】

明·张鼐

自余客京师扫一室，与俞子叔和榻相对也。旅舍无事，焚香读书，读倦则就榻，少则复读，乐此以为常。叔和常与余论息，至今犹能记忆之。归而破屋数椽，几邻灶下，斗室湫溢不通，宾客愧余息之无地也，已复笑曰："息因地乎哉？"孟子云：日夜所息。人以鼻气之出为息，凡物以发荣润泽为滋息生息。则知息者，生气而非止气也，如宿火于灰，灰暖而火活，传薪则然矣，是满炉都是然体也。若止气为息，如灯一拨，更无留焰，是死法矣。今俗人作梦是也。孟子说个日夜便是个通乎昼夜而知。须知此气时

175

明·文徵明 古木寒泉图

时出，时时入，如日月之代明，潮夕之往来，即其息处，纯是生生不已机括就，出作时亦自有入息在，非专以入为息也。有道之人日日应酬，俱有个安顿道理，忙时能暇，烦时能简。阳明先生师旅倥偬，尚自讲学不辍，此非出作时是入息乎？草木郁于花果而晦于根，宁一刻不发生，宁一刻不息也？只是草木自花果至根，通是元气流转，元气不全，生亦不生，息亦不息矣。人生须是完全个元气。所谓敬以持之，定静安虑，皆从敬出，敬则无思，敬则无事，无思无事，是事物主宰。所谓万境自闹，人心自闲，看得闲心，便觉境亦不闹。安见息因乎地也？今不求息地，但求息本。自昼至夜，遇事烦扰，能不忙乱否？梦境能清彻否？言语能不多费否？意气能不发扬太过否？知见能脱洒不横据否？合则便是生息，所谓日用，皆是元气精炼，如以炭养火也；不合则攘攘时已耗散略尽，虽瞑目危坐，亦是沉昏不得言息。大抵世人只凭滋味养得血气，口体所需与百为所耗，仅足相当。夜卧骚扰神明，遂令梦境多惊多惧，或白昼宴居尸寝，便与离魂壳子一般。今人以庄严净室卧离魂壳子于中，毕竟有何活意？所以谚云"闾门巷里好读书"，盖真读书者也。叔和常言设榻于坐侧，凡交际、诵读、著述、游戏，倦则一息，或友朋过谭，谈久亦相对而息，此亦一小安乐法也。龙溪先生曰："至人有息无睡息。"气活而睡，则游魂百出矣，正于作处观息，乃大安乐法也。作息机说。

Tales with Morals

From *Shuehtao Shiaoshu*

Chiang Chinchih
c. 1600

Once a general was shot in the head with an arrow in battle, and he quickly ran home to have the arrow pulled out.

He asked a surgeon, which in Chinese is called "an external doctor," to treat him.

The surgeon examined it and, taking a pair of scissors, cut the arrow off as close to the skin as possible, and asked for his fee.

"Please take out the arrow for me, for it is inside my head, and I am going to die of it!" pleaded the general.

"I am an external doctor," replied the surgeon. "What has that got to do with me? I have done my part. You can ask a doctor of internal medicine to attend to the rest of it."

The general did not know what to do.

Moral: The authorities today who shirk their responsibilities and pass them on to the next official are of the opinion that the arrow inside should be left to the doctor of internal medicine.

There was a quack doctor who advertised that he could cure the camel of his hump. Someone brought a camel to him to be cured.

The doctor placed a wooden board on the ground and made the camel lie on it. Then he placed another wooden board on top of the animal and made people go on top and stamp on it as hard as they could.

The camel died of it.

The owner of the camel went to sue him at court for killing the camel.

The camel doctor said: "I am a camel doctor. My business is to make humps straight. It is none of my business whether the animal remains alive."

Moral: The magistrates who see to it that the taxes are collected properly, but do not see to it that the people remain alive, are in no way different from the camel doctor.

There was once a poor man who picked up a hen's egg.

He brought the egg home and said to his wife:

"Look here, I have found a fortune!"

And he showed the egg to his wife, and said:

"This is my fortune, but you have to wait about ten years. I will have a neighbor's hen sit on this egg, and when the chicken grows up, I shall possess a hen. The hen will lay fifteen eggs a month, which means fifteen chickens. In two years' time, we shall have three hundred chickens, for which we shall get ten dollars. With these ten dollars, I will buy five calves, and when these grow up and bear other calves, I shall have twenty-five cows in three years. When these multiply, in another three years we shall have a hundred and fifty cows, which will sell for three hundred dollars. I will loan the three hundred dollars for interest, and in another three years, we shall have at least five hundred dollars. Then I shall spend two thirds of this sum on a house and farm, and one third of it for buying servants and a concubine, and live happily for life."

When his wife heard him mention the word "concubine," she became very angry and smashed the egg to pieces, shouting, "I will not tolerate this seed of all evil!"

The husband was also very angry, and he went to sue his wife at court, the charge being that she had broken up his fortune, and was consequently a bad wife. He asked that the wife be severely punished, and told the magistrate the whole story.

"But," said the magistrate, "your wife stopped you when you had come only to the concubine: you hadn't quite finished telling her what you were going to do yet."

"Indeed, I had finished, Your Honor," said the husband.

"But no," said the magistrate, "your concubine was going to have a son, who would pass the official examinations, become an official, and bring you great honor. Is all this nothing to you? To think that such a huge fortune should be smashed by the fist of a bad woman. She shall be killed!"

"But this was only a discussion; why should I be sentenced to death for it?" protested the wife.

"Your husband's buying a concubine was only a discussion also. Why should you be jealous?"

"That is right, too, Your Honor," said the woman. "But to forestall an evil, you have to nip it in the bud."

The magistrate was delighted and set her free.

Moral: To know that a thing does not exist is the best way to forget the desire for it.

The Solicitor for Contributions

A robber and a monk met a tiger on a mountain path. The robber got ready his bow and arrow to attack the tiger, but that seemed to produce no effect on the tiger, who steadily advanced nearer in spite of the robber's threatening arrow. In that desperate situation, the monk, who held in his hand a book of receipts for soliciting contributions to his temple, threw the book at the tiger and the tiger ran away. Back in his cave, the tiger cub asked its father, "Why are you not afraid of the robber but of the monk?" And the old tiger replied, "Because I could fight with the robber when he came near, but what was I to do if the monk approached me for contributions?"

The Quack Doctor

One day a quack doctor killed a fat patient. The family of the deceased wanted to sue him, but the affair was finally settled by the doctor undertaking to bury the dead man at his own cost. The quack doctor, however, was very poor himself, and being unable to hire people, he undertook to bury the corpse himself with the help of his wife and two children. The corpse weighed about two hundred pounds, and they had to make frequent stops on the journey. When they bent to pick up the corpse again, the wife remarked to her husband, "My dear husband, next time you go out curing patients, you should pick a thin one."

The Cuckoo

There was a fool whose wife had a lover. Once he came back at night, and as the lover was trying to leap through the window, he caught one of his shoes. This he put under his pillow thinking that he would use it as evidence and prosecute his wife at court next day. During his sleep, however, his wife secretly exchanged it with one of her husband's own shoes. On waking up next morning, the husband looked carefully at the shoe and finding it to be his own, apologized to his wife, "I am very sorry for last night. I didn't know it was I myself who jumped out of the window."

The Miser

There was a certain miser who, hearing about the reputation of a greater miser than himself, went to the other miser's home to become his disciple. As usual, he had to bring some present to his new master and brought with him a bowl of water with a piece of paper cut in the form of a fish. The great miser happened to be away from home and his wife received him. "Here is my fish as a humble present from your new pupil," remarked the visitor. The miser's wife received it with thanks and brought up an empty cup and asked him to have tea. After the pupil had pretended to drink tea, the miser's wife again asked him to help himself to the cakes by drawing two circles in the air with her hand. In came the master miser and when he saw his wife drawing two circles, he shouted to her, "What extravagance! You are giving two cakes away! A semi-circle should do!"

The Henpecked Husband

One day a wife was very angry with her henpecked husband and wanted to torture him with a special instrument for cracking finger bones. There being no such finger-cracker at home, she sent her husband to borrow it from a neighbor. The husband was grumbling all the way as he passed out of the house, considering it as adding insult to injury. "What are you grumbling at?" shouted the wife. The husband was frightened and immediately turned around and said, "I was only saying that we should buy a finger-cracker and keep it at home."

【 雪 涛 谐 史 （ 节 录 ） 】

明·江盈科

……又有医者，自称善外科，一禆将阵回，中流矢，深入膜内，延使治。乃持并州剪，剪去矢管，跪而请谢。禆将曰："镞在膜内者须亟治。"医曰："此内科事，不应并责我。"噫，脚入邻家，然犹我之脚也；镞在膜内，然亦医者之事也。乃隔一壁，辄思委脚；隔一膜，辄欲分科。然则痛安能已、责安能诿乎？今日当事诸公，见事之不可为，而但因循苟安，以遗来者，亦若委痛于邻家，推责于内科之意。

昔有医人，自媒能治背驼，曰："如弓者，如虾者，如曲环者，延吾治，可朝治而夕如矢。"一人信焉，而使治驼。乃索板二片，以一置地下，卧驼者其上，又以一压焉，而脚蹒焉。驼者随直，亦复随死。其子欲鸣诸官，医人曰："我业治驼，但管人直，那管人死？"呜呼！世之为令，但管钱粮完，不管百姓死，何以异于此医也哉！

妄心

见卵求夜，庄周以为早计；及观恒人之情，更有早计于庄周者。一市人贫甚，朝不谋夕。偶一日拾得一鸡卵，喜而告其妻曰："我有家当矣。"妻问安在，持卵示之，曰："此是。然须十年，家当乃就。"因与妻计曰："我持此卵，借邻人伏鸡乳之，待彼雏成，就中取一雌者，归而生卵，一月可得十五鸡，两年之内，鸡又生鸡，可得鸡三百，堪易十金。我以十金易五牸，牸复生牸，三年可得二十五牛，牸所生者，又复生牸，三年可得百五十牛，堪易三百金矣。吾持此金举责，三年间，半千金可得也。就中以三之二市田宅，以三之一市僮仆，买小妻，我乃与尔优游以终余年，不亦快乎？"妻闻欲买小妻，怫然大怒，以手击鸡卵碎之，曰："毋留祸种。"夫怒挞其妻，乃质于官，曰："立败我家者，此恶妇也，请诛之。"官司问家何在？败何状？其人历数自鸡卵起，至小妻止。官司曰："尔家当尚未说完。"其人曰："完矣。"官曰："尔小妻生子，读书登科，出仕取富贵，独不入算耶？如许大家当，碎于恶妇一拳，真可诛。"命烹之。妻号曰："夫所言皆未然事，奈何见烹？"官司曰："你夫言买妾，亦未然事，奈何见妒？"妇曰："固然，第除祸欲蚤耳。"官笑而释之。

噫，兹人之计利，贪心也；其妻之毁卵，妒心也；总之，皆妄心也。知其为妄，泊然无嗜，颓然无起，即见在者，且属诸幻，况未来乎！嘻，世之妄意早计，希图非望者，独一算鸡卵之人乎？

化缘

一强盗与化缘僧遇虎于途。盗持弓御虎，虎犹近前而不肯退。僧不得已，持缘薄掷虎前，虎骇而退。虎之子问虎曰："不畏盗，乃畏僧乎？"虎曰："盗来，我与格斗。僧问我化缘，我将甚么打发他？"

庸医

又一庸医，治一肥汉而死，其家难之，曰："我饶你，不告状，但为我我葬埋。"医人贫甚，率其妻与二子共抬，至中途，力不能举。乃吟诗曰："自祖相传历世医，"妻续云："丈夫为事连累妻。"长子续云："可奈尸肥抬不动，"次子续云："这遭只选瘦人医。"

有痴夫者其妻与人私

有痴夫者，其妻与人私。一日，撞遇奸夫于室，跳窗逸去，只夺其鞋一只，用以枕头，曰："平明往质于官。"妻乘其睡熟，即以夫所着鞋易之。明日，夫起，细视其鞋，乃己鞋也，因谢妻曰："我错怪了你，昨日跳出窗的，原来就是我。"

有习悭术者

一人已习悭术，犹谓未足，乃从悭师学其术。往见之，但用纸剪鱼，盛水一瓶，故名曰酒，为学悭贽礼。偶值悭师外出，惟妻在家，知其来学之意，并所执贽仪，乃使一婢用空盏传出曰："请茶。"实无茶也。又以两手作一圈曰："请饼。"如是而已。学悭者既出，悭师乃归，其妻悉述其事以告。悭师作色曰："何乃费此厚款？"随用手作半圈样曰："只这半边饼，觳打发他。"

惧内者

有惧内者，见怒于妻，将掭其指。夫云："家无掭具。"妻命从邻家借用。夫往借时，低声怨咨，妻唤回，问曰："适口中作何语？"夫答曰："我道这刑具，也须自家置一副。"

On Love

"On Heroes and Women"

Chou Chuan

c. 1600

It is often said that "the great heroes of history met their match in women." By this people mean that the love of a woman is a dangerous thing and that such episodes somehow take away from our idea of a "hero." One must keep away from the snares and temptations of women. And so forth.

I beg to differ. I think what makes heroes heroes is that they have love in a greater measure than others and are capable of greater devotion to something, with their heart and soul in it. Only those who can make great sacrifices can love truly. All the universe comes from love. Where the heart dictates, a man guides his life by it. It is not confined to any one thing, but runs through all human affairs, beginning with the love of woman. Love and devotion can be just as well applied to a national cause, to friendship, to the business in hand. Therefore the *Book of Songs* [edited by Confucius] did not regard the love between man and woman as sin, and the *Book of Changes* spoke of marriage as fulfilling "the heart of the universe." We can run through the great names of history in our mind and find that not one of them did not have a great love. There was Shiang Yu. What a warrior and what a man! When he found himself surrounded by the enemy and the end was near, he got up in his tent, wrote some verse, and sang with his sweetheart, and they wept together before killing themselves with a sword. And his enemy, too, who became the First Emperor of Han, had an unsuspected tenderness. Assuredly he was a great warrior who scolded his generals like boys. He then became emperor, but before his death, he said to his queen, "Dance for me, dear, the folk dance of our home country and I shall sing for you our folk songs." Thus an emperor died.

I therefore say that it takes a man with a great heart to have a great love affair. I have noticed that those who made good as scholars and writers loved certain things to the exclusion of everything else. And when a crisis arose, these people acted with decision and firmness and showed a strength of character above the others. When the country called, they responded. There is no mystery about it. They had a big *heart*, and merely transferred that great love from one thing to something else. Therefore, as I say, love is not confined to any one thing. Only those who make some great sacrifice can love truly.

I am sure that the heart can shake a throne. It is the wholeness of love that accomplishes great things in this universe. Here we are dealing with a vital force that cold philosophers in their gray plaster walls little know. One thinks of Nelson and Napoleon. The greatest emperor in all China's history, whose reign is conceded by all to be the best, was Tang Taitsung (reigned, A.D. 627-649), the real founder of the great Tang Dynasty. I like the episode of his love for his twelve-year-old princess, nicknamed "Bizon." When the little girl died, he was unconsoled and lost his appetite for a whole month. He explained to his servants who urged him to eat, "I love this child so much. I can't get over it. I don't know why." Is it not our weakness that makes our strength?

【 英雄气短说 】

明·周铨

　　或者曰：儿女情深，英雄气短，以言乎情，不可恃也。情溺则气损，气损则英雄之分亦亏。故夫人溺情不返，有至大杀而无余。甚矣，情之不可恃有如是也！

　　周子曰：非也。夫天下无大存者，必不能大割；有大忘者，其始必有大不忍；故天下一情所聚也。情之所在，一往辄深：移以事君，事君忠；以交友，交友信；以处事，处事深。故《国风》许人好色，《易》称归妹见天地之心。凡所谓情，政非一节之称也，通于人道之大，发端儿女之间。古未有不深于情，能大其英雄之气者。以项王暗哑叱咤，为汉军所窘，则夜起帐中，慷慨为诗，与美人倚歌而和，泣数行下。

明·唐寅　吹箫仕女图

汉高雄才谩骂，呼大将如小儿，及威加海内，病卧床席，召戚夫人与泣曰："若为我楚舞，吾为若楚歌。"歌数阕，一恸欲绝。嗟夫！此其气力绝人，皆有拔山跨海之概，乃亦不能不失声儿女子之一顾！他若如姬于魏信陵，夷光于范少伯，卓文君于司马相如，数君子者皆飘飘有凌云之致。乃一笑功成，五湖风月；与后之自着犊鼻，与庸保杂作，涤器于市，前后相映。呜呼！情之移人，一至是哉！余故谓惟儿女情深，乃不为英雄气短。尝观古来能读书善文章者，其始皆有不屑之事，后乃有不测之功。触白刃，死患难，一旦乘时大作，义不返顾，是岂所置之殊乎？竭情以往，亦举此以措云尔。余故曰：天下有大割者，必有所大存，盖不系于一节而言也。乃后世有拥阿娇，思贮金屋，曰"吾情也"，噫！乌足语此！

Cut Flowers and Vases

Chang Tehchien[1]

c. 1600

Many authorities have written on this subject, including Tu Chihshui and Yuan Chunglang. The following is probably the best connected summary. On the more fascinating subject of arranging miniature landscapes, the best is still that by Shen Fu, the author of *Six Chapters of a Floating Life*. Su Tungpo has a piece about a miniature landscape arrangement in his home, inherited from his father. No dates of Chang Tehchien can be found, but this piece bears a preface dated 1595.

1. Vases

The selection of a proper vase for flowers is the first step. There are elements of season, copper vases for winter and spring, and porcelain for summer and fall, and elements of size and space,

---

[1] 明代学者张谦德——编者注。

big ones for big halls and small ones for a studio or library. Copper is preferred to gold and silver to avoid suggestion of opulence, and vases with earrings should be avoided, as also a symmetrical arrangement in pairs, to avoid their looking as if on a temple altar. The vases should be more slender at the top than the bottom for steadiness.

In general, slender and small vases are preferred to the wide and big. The best is four or five inches[2] or six or seven inches, one foot being the maximum. If the vase is too small, the flowers will not keep for long.

Copper [or bronze] vessels that can be used for holding flowers are jars, bottles, goblets, and pots formerly used for holding wine but quite suitable for this use.

Antique copper [and bronze] vases and bowls or alms bowls

----

[2] The Chinese foot contains ten inches, or 14.1 English inches. "Five inches" means half a Chinese foot, or seven inches by English measurements.

which have been found underground are especially suitable, for from their long burial underground there has been a change from contact with the soil. They keep flowers as fresh as on the bough, so that they last longer and wither more slowly. Some flowers even start to form seeds in the pot, especially when the bases are very old and the water used is excellent. Earthenware which has lain buried for a thousand years acts in the same way.

There were no porcelain [*tzu*] vessels in ancient times till the Tang Period (beginning in the seventh century), and only copper [or bronze] was used. The use of kiln ceramics began with Tang.[3] Later came [the products known by their *yao* or kilns of] Chai, Ju, Ko, Ting, Lungchuan, Chunchow, Changsheng, Wuni, Shuanteh, and Chenghua. Thus a great variety of chinaware has developed. In point of antiquity, the

---

[3] Practically no one has seen a Tang porcelain, by which is meant high-fired enamel-coated vessels. The Chinese earthenware dated back to prehistoric times. But already in A.D. 950, we have the famous Chai ware, extremely thin and delicate, which presupposes an earlier development. The chinaware mentioned here begins with Chai and ends with Chenghua (1465-1487).

bronze or copper vessels would be best. Among the porcelain, Chai and Ju [Chaiyao and Juyao] are priceless because they do not exist any more. Therefore the Kuanyao, Koyao, Shuanteh, and Tingyao rank among the best and most valuable today. The Lungchuan [Celadon], Changsheng, Wuni, and Chenghua rank next.[4]

There are ancient bronze jars, and Lungchuan and Chunchow vases of a very big size, two or three feet high, which have no other use. In winter, they can be used for big sprays of the plum flower, but sulfur must be thrown into the water [to prevent cracking from ice formations].

2. Different Flowers, Graded for Beauty

[omitted]

---

[4] Koyao and Kuanyao are Sung. In general, Sung ware (twelfth century) is monochrome, sometimes bluish green, like Kuanyao or Lungchuan, but especially valued is its white, such as Tingyao, with faint marking of different kinds. Bright-colored porcelain was introduced in the Ming wares, such as Shuanteh and Chenghua (fifteenth century).

3. Cutting

Flowers should be cut from near-by gardens in early morning with the dew on them, chosen from the half-blooms. Thus their fragrance and color will keep for several days. If cut after the sun is high up and the dew is gone, they will last only one or two days, besides having less brilliance and fragrance.

In cutting flowers, choose the twig for its bend and posture, perhaps fuller on top than below, weighted on the right or on the left, or curling together, or straggling and curving in one direction. Or a branch may perhaps stand out boldly alone, full and round both on top and below. In putting them in the vase, see that they bend or turn up, or incline or stand straight, in a harmonious grouping and height, so that each seems to say something, such as the postures chosen by artists for painting. Thus their natural beauty may be preserved. A straight, full, and shaggy twig of flowers cannot be considered in this art of *chingkung* [vase arrangements].

All flowers whether grown on trees or grass can be used for vases. But in picking them, soft branches must be picked with the hand, while stiff boughs must be cut with shears. A lover of flowers will bear this in mind.

Stiff branches (suggesting rugged strength or character) are easy to choose. The most difficult to choose are flowers from grass bushes. Unless one has seen a great many famous paintings, the arrangement easily becomes common.

4. Vase Arrangements

As soon as a branch is cut, it should be quickly put in a vase with a small neck, which must be stuffed up to keep the vital force [*chi*] contained in it. Thus it will last several days.

Generally, the flowers should match with the vase in size, being slightly higher than it. For example, if the vase is one foot, the flowers should stand one foot and three or four inches from its mouth. If the vase is six or seven inches, the flowers should show eight or nine inches, to give an agreeable effect. If too high, the jar easily topples over, and if too low, the arrangement will lack elegance.

With flowers for small vases, the idea is that they should look slender and well formed, and should never be stuffy or over-crowded. If only one branch is placed, choose one which has an enticing posture with a twisting movement. If two branches are placed, one must be lower than the other, with the effect that they seem to come out from the same branch, or so arrange them that each branch faces a certain direction and they seem to fit in as one living branch. A binding twine must be used to fix their relative positions.

Although one always tries to avoid a stuffy effect, it is equally true that there must not be too few or too small flowers for the vase. Where such is the case, surround it with small slender twigs around the base of the arrangement. That will save the situation.

Only one or two kinds of flowers should be used for one vase.
A little mixture of more kinds will make the arrangement
confusing and disagreeable. Exceptions here are the autumn
flowers.

5. Feeding and Care

Flowers in nature get their nourishment from the dew.
Therefore one should best use rain water, which is similar in
nature to the dew. In some cases, honey or boiled water may
be used. The artist must suit the nourishment to the particular
needs.

The first important thing is to have a jar of collected rain water.
In default of this, clear water from a lake of river may be used.
Well water should be avoided because it contains salt and is bad
for the flowers.

The water in the vase mostly contains poison. Therefore the
water should be changed every morning to make the flowers

last. They wither easily in two or three days if the water is not changed.

At night, the vase may stand in the open where it is sheltered from wind. Thus it will keep for several days. This is like *ginseng* [root for long life] provided by nature.

6. Special Needs of Different Flowers

The dark plum flower[5]—cauterize the point where it is cut, and wrap it up with clay.

---

[5] I have never seen this flower abroad. The fruit is of the dark plum variety. There are two Chinese kinds, the *li*, which is light-colored, and the *mei*, which is dark. This flower of the *Prunus* genus is highly prized not only because it blooms in snow with pale pink flowers, but also because it has a singular beauty in having stiff and slightly twisted branches, and flowers standing on the branch without leaves, suggesting cool independence of spirit, pointing out straight into the cool air. It has also a very subtle fragrance. Chinese poetry and paintings associate it with moonlight shadows and snow. Its elegance of posture is similar to a twig of quince, or to forsythia which has light yellow blossoms like *lamei*, which is winter sweet.

The tree peony [*mutan*]—heat the broken joint with lamplight until it is soft.

The gardenia—lightly hammer its roots until they are frayed, and rub in a little salt.

The lotus—tie up the bottom with tangled hair and wrap it up in a ball of clay.

The cherry apple—wrap the bottom up with mint leaves and soak it in water.

Outside these few kinds, flowers can be cut and placed in vases without more ado. The tree peony takes honey well, and the honey will not be affected by it. By using boiled water with bamboo twigs, the hollyhock, the touch-me-not, and the Indian lotus, the leaves will not wither [easily?].

7. Things to Avoid

Generally there are six things to avoid: (a) use of well water, (b) neglect in changing water, (c) handling with greasy hands, (d) injury by cats and mice, (e) contact with tobacco smoke or lamp smoke, and (f) a completely closed room with no movement of air. Any one of these things is bad for the flowers.

8. Protection of the Vase

In winter [when the water in a vase may freeze] there are no good flowers except the narcissus, the winter sweet [*lamei*], and the dark plum [*mei*]. Here wide-mouthed vessels, like ancient wine goblets or wine jars, should be used, and an inner tube made of tin placed inside it containing water for the flowers so as to avoid cracking. When a small vase is used, put some sulfur in the water and keep it near a southern window near the sun in the daytime and put it near the bed at night to prevent freezing. Another way is to use unsalted meat juice, having taken care to remove the fat first. Thus the flowers will blossom without injury to the container.

When boiled water is used for certain flowers, first keep a certain amount in an ordinary jar, keeping its mouth closed tightly. Wait until it is cool, then put it into the vase with rain water so that the vase will not crack. Be sure to remember this, or a valuable vase may be so spoiled.

【 瓶花谱 】

明·张谦德

品瓶

　　凡插贮花，先须择瓶。春、冬用铜，秋、夏用磁。因乎时也。堂厦宜大，书室宜小，因乎地也。贵磁、铜，贱金、银，尚清雅也。忌有环，忌成对，像神祠也。口欲小而足欲厚，取其安稳而不泄气也。

　　大都瓶宁瘦毋过壮，宁小毋过大。极高者不可过一尺，得六七寸，四五寸瓶插贮，佳。若太小，则养花又不能太久。

铜器之可用插花者，曰尊，曰罍，曰瓶，曰壶。古人原用贮酒，今取以插花极似合宜。

古铜瓶、钵，入土年久，受土气深，以之养花，花色鲜明如枝头，开速而谢迟，或谢则就瓶结实。若水锈、传世古则尔。陶器入土千年亦然。

古无磁瓶，皆以铜为之。至唐始尚窑器，厥后有柴、汝、官、哥、定、龙泉、均州、章生、乌泥、宣、成等窑，而品类多矣。尚古莫如铜器，窑则柴、汝最贵，而世绝无之。官、哥、宣、定，为当今第一珍品。而龙泉、均州、章生、乌泥、成化等瓶，亦以次见重矣。

瓷器以各式古壶、胆瓶、尊、觚、一枝瓶，为书室中妙品。次则小蓍草瓶、纸槌瓶、圆素瓶、鹅颈壁瓶，皆可供插花之用。余如暗花、茄袋、葫芦样、细口匾肚瘦足药坛等瓶，俱不入清供。

古铜壶，龙泉、均州瓶，有极大高二三尺者，别无可用，冬日投以硫黄、斫大枝梅花插供亦得。

品花

《花经》九命升降，吾家先哲（君讳翊）所制，可谓缩万象于笔端、实幻景于片楮矣。今谱瓶花，例当列品，录其入供者得数十种，亦以九品九命次第之。

一品九命：兰，牡丹，梅，蜡梅，各色细叶菊，水仙，滇茶，瑞香，菖阳。

二品八命：蕙，酴醾，西府海棠，宝珠茉莉，黄白山茶，岩桂，白菱，松枝，含笑，茶花。

三品七命：芍药，各色千叶桃，莲，丁香，蜀茶，竹。

四品六命：山矾，夜合，赛兰，蔷薇，秋海棠，锦葵，杏，辛夷，各色千叶榴，佛桑，梨。

五品五命：玫瑰，蔷卜，紫薇，金萱，忘忧，豆蔻。

六品四命：玉兰，迎春，芙蓉，素馨，柳芽，茶梅。

七品三命：金雀，踯躅，枸杞，金凤，千叶李，枳壳，杜鹃。

八品二命：千叶戎葵，玉簪，鸡冠，洛阳，林禽，秋葵。

九品一命：剪春罗，剪秋罗，高良姜，石菊，牵牛，木瓜，淡竹叶。

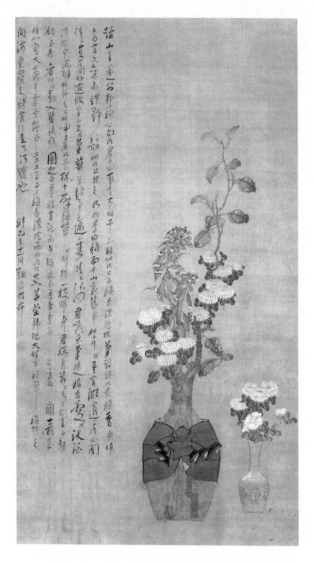

明·陈洪绶　瓶花图

折枝

　　折取花枝，须得家园邻圃，侵晨带露，择其半开者折供，则香色数日不减。若日高露晞折得者，不特香不全、色不鲜，且一两日即萎落矣。

　　凡折花须择枝，或上茸下瘦，或左高右低，右高左低。或两蟠台接，偃亚偏曲。或挺露一干中出，上簇下蕃，铺盖瓶口。取俯仰高下，疏密斜正，各具异意态，全得画家折技花景象，方有天趣。若直枝篷头花朵，不入清供。

　　花不论草木，皆可供瓶中插贮。第摘取有二法：取柔枝也，宜手摘；取劲干也，宜剪却。惜花人亦须识得。采折劲枝尚易取巧，独草花最难摘取，非熟玩名人写生画迹，似难脱俗。

插贮

折得花枝，急须插入小口瓶中，紧紧塞之，勿泄其气，则数日可玩。

大率插花须要花与瓶称，令花稍高于瓶。假如瓶高一尺，花出瓶口一尺三四寸；瓶高六七寸，花出瓶口八九寸，乃佳。忌太高，太高瓶易仆；忌太低，太低雅趣失。

小瓶插花宜瘦巧，不宜繁杂。若止插一枝，须择枝柯奇古、屈曲斜袅者。欲插二种，须分高下合插，俨若一枝天生者；或两枝彼此各向，先凑簇像生，用麻丝缚定插之。

瓶花虽忌繁冗，尤忌花瘦于瓶。须折斜欹花枝，铺撒小瓶左右，乃为得体也。瓶中插花，止可一种、两种。稍过多便冗杂可厌，独秋花不尔也。

滋养

凡花滋雨露以生，故瓶中养花，宜用天水，亦取雨露之意。更有宜蜂蜜者，宜沸汤者。清赏之士，贵随材而造就焉。滋养第一雨水，宜多蓄听用。不得已则用清净江湖水。井水味咸，养花不茂，勿用。插花之水，类有小毒，须旦旦换之，花乃可久。若两三日不换，花辄零落。瓶花每至夜间，宜择无风处露之，可观数日，此天与人参之术也。

事宜

梅花初折，宜火烧折处，固渗以泥。牡丹初折，宜灯燃折处，待软乃歇。蔷卜花初折，宜捶碎其根，擦盐少许。荷花初折，宜乱发缠根，取泥封窍。海棠初折，薄荷嫩叶包根入水。除此数种，可任意折插，不必拘泥。牡丹花宜蜜养，蜜乃不坏。竹枝、戎葵、金凤、芙蓉用沸汤插枝，叶乃不萎。

花忌

瓶花之忌，大概有六：一者，井水插贮；二者，久不换水；三者，油手拈弄；四者，猫、鼠伤残；五者，香、烟、灯煤熏触；六者，密室闭藏，不沾风露。有一于此，俱为瓶花之病。

护瓶

冬间别无嘉卉，仅有水仙、蜡梅、梅花数种而已。此时极宜敞口古尊、罍插贮，须用锡作替管盛水，可免破裂之患。若欲用小磁瓶插贮，必投以硫黄少许，日置南窗下近日色，夜置卧榻，旁俾近人气，亦可不冻。一法：用淡肉法，去浮油入瓶插花，则花悉开而瓶略无损。瓶花有宜沸汤者，须以寻常瓶贮汤插之，紧塞其口，候既冷，方以佳瓶盛雨水易却，庶不损瓶。若即用佳瓶贮沸汤，必伤珍重之器矣，戒之。

Hints to Hosts and Guests

Shen Chungying
c. 1600?

> A great many treatises bearing this name (*Shangcheng*) and
> relating to wine dinners have been written, among which I
> select the following as the best.

One should drink within one's limits when on an excursion to
dangerous high places, when on a voyage, when the ground is
full of thistles, when something important has to be attended
to on the morrow, when traveling alone without servants, and
when recently recovered from an illness.

Sometimes a host spends a great deal of money on food and
fails to provide good wine. Would it not be more sensible to
save some money from the food and provide good wine?

The object of a friendly dinner is to enjoy oneself. Sometimes while a wine game is going on, a guest does not pay attention, and when it comes to his turn, he is at a complete loss as to what it is all about, which spoils the fun.

Sometimes a host counts on some guests not turning up and arranges the places accordingly. An awkward situation arises when there are more guests than places for them, causing last-minute confusion, which is damnable.

Guests should leave when it is just right. Some guests overstay their welcome, causing great inconvenience to the host and his servants. This is especially hard in extreme cold or hot weather.

Wine served at dinner should be uniform. Sometimes strong wine is followed by light, or the two come together mixed or improperly warmed up. This is considered bad service.

To descend upon a dinner uninvited or without being expected is permissible only among the best of friends. Sometimes such intrusion is disgusting, particularly when associated with taking too much liberty. The guests can only wink at each other to show their disgust. Why does anyone want to lose his self-respect?

There are people whom you have never met at dinners but who grow suddenly very hospitable because they want to ask you a favor. After their object is accomplished, they forget all about you again. Such people should be avoided.

One cannot feel too happy about a party where the guests break up in a hurry, perhaps on account of rain or snow, or because of a long distance to travel, or to get into the city before the closing time.

It is not nice to see some guests nibble at the fruit or cold dishes before the others have come. But it may be the host's fault when a dinner is held up because the guest of honor is late and the host fails to give something to quell the hunger for his first guests.

I do not know when the finger-guessing game started. But it is just a pastime, enjoyable only when people do not cheat in timing or use tricks. Otherwise, it is not worth while.

Good servants help to attend to the service and can follow intelligently a wine game. Servants who steal food or drinks, or are uncouth and rude, or have disgusting manners, only spoil the dinner.

It is a pity when there is a good wine game and no worthy participants, or when a good drinker does not find one with equal capacity to keep him company.

Sometimes a guest is fined to drink, but cannot take it. He begs to be allowed to drink the next time, which is a good idea for both host and guest. Sometimes the officer of the game insists on his drinking until the man throws up. This is very silly.

I do not approve of a host who does not urge his guests to drink or fails to provide dice, nor do I approve of stuffy guests who are strict on principles and refuse to take part in wine games.

There are some people who give a dinner in expectation of being invited in return and who like to compare the lavishness of dinners, as if their lives depended upon such trifles. That is a form of vulgarity.

Guests and host should be neither too formal nor too informal. Some guests decline to take even a low seat and hold up the dinner with their false modesty, or a host provides a too meager dinner while he gorges himself without regard to his guests. This is damnable.

Sometimes guests meet those who are from different professions. They make themselves ridiculous by dropping names or talking about their official affairs. The same thing is true of successful candidates of the government examinations who like to harp about their taking degrees.

If a host cannot drink himself, he should ask some of the guests who can to take his place at dinner to prevent the dinner from getting too dull. There is not much fun in sitting to a sumptuous dinner in a freezing atmosphere.

Some rich or influential people make a show of cordiality at dinner and make all sorts of promises which they promptly forget. Some other people try to ingratiate themselves at table. Both kinds are despicable.

It is a point of bad manners when the guests leave each other after dinner without a friendly feeling, or do not offer to take those without transportation in their carriages or boats. But of course drunken guests or objectionable persons should be avoided.

One should not treat monks when they are at table any differently from the others or make fun of their religion. It is neither good form nor sensible behavior.

There may be less well-read persons among the guests. One should not be too critical of them. For men are born differently, some more intelligent than others. A cultured man will be nice to all.

One should guard against using unrefined language, or use of abusive language, or misbehaving under the pretense of drunkenness, or making a scene.

Some people are too free and easy and keep on demanding more and more of the food which they like. This is bad manners.

One should have regard for one's neighbors at table. Some guests spread their arms about and drink like oxen without regard for those sitting next to them. Such conduct is hateful.

A cultured gentleman tries to avoid the following: incoherent and silly talk when drunk, putting things back on the plate, pouring wine back into the bottle, bringing too many attendants with him without consideration for the host.

Excuse and allowance must be made for a host on busy occasions like a wedding or a funeral when he cannot be expected to attend to all details of the guests' comfort.

A birthday is, according to the ancients, a painful day of labor for the mother. On such a day, or when celebrating a baby's first full month, one should try not to be extravagant, and should avoid slaughter of animals, as a religious consideration.

When a party is held in a garden, it is bad manners to allow the servants to pick flowers and fruit and break branches.

Rich men seldom invite their poor relatives to dinner. But when they meet another wealthy person, or a V.I.P. or a notorious racketeer or a popular courtesan, they entertain most lavishly. It is their folly.

Snobs show themselves at once at dinner parties. It is seen in the way they listen to and show respect to some important guest, or even to a vulgar, illiterate millionaire. Or some young people show no respect for elders or behave as if they were not present. These are all signs of lack of culture.

There are dinners given when one does not pause to reflect how sad it is, such as a dinner given to yamen runners and employees during a lawsuit, when the host perhaps has to sell his child to provide such entertainment. Equally sad is the dinner given by a squanderer of a family fortune, without the host realizing how sad it really is.

Sometimes the guests become very uncomfortable when the wine games are too strictly carried out by the umpire, or badly carried out, with the result that good drinkers have no chance to drink and others are made to drink beyond their capacity. Or sometimes the umpire is not at his job and lets everything go to pieces.

It can happen that a guest of honor cannot drink. He must exercise restraint upon himself and allow others to enjoy themselves.

At wedding dinners, one should be especially careful to see that one does not bring along servants who may make drunken scenes. The same is true of dinners given by families involved in a lawsuit.

It is necessary to have an umpire or presiding officer to see that wine games proceed in order, especially when there are many guests. But it is not proper to have another deputy umpire, or even a supervisor to supervise the presiding officer.

It is a most exasperating thing to have to send servants to urge invited guests to come who will not come until they are sent for again and again. From noon till sundown, the servants run till their legs are tired, those looking for their appearance wait until their eyes are tired, the other guests wait in hunger, and the host is embarrassed about whether to ask the guests to be seated at table or not.

Guests are sometimes invited to meet a guest of honor, and the host depends upon their co-operation. Sometimes guests who have been notified in time arrive late after the guest of honor, or others join in making cruel demands upon the host. Such drunks are beneath contempt.

It is also annoying to see a host unprepared or short of things when the guests have arrived.

Dinner should be given according to one's means and station. One can foretell that a well-to-do family which is unduly stingy with its food cannot amount to much in the future, and also that a common scholar who is too extravagant is not going to keep up for long.

At a dinner with new relatives or children, one should not talk of poetry and history, which will embarrass those who cannot follow.

One gives dinners and entertainments according to what is suitable to one's means. One should not waste, nor just blindly follow custom. To be stingy when one should spend and to spend when it is not necessary are both out of place.

A man sometimes promises gifts or dinners when he is drunk and forgets all about it. And he may make this into a habit. He is not conscious of it, but to others he can be very tiring.

It does not speak of good manners when one is a vegetarian and does not make it known until he is seated at table and refuses to touch this or that. Then the host or the other guests find out, and it puts the host in a most awkward position of having to produce something suitable on the spot.

A dinner may become very dull when there is no challenge to drink among the guests. On the other hand, when two guests get too engrossed in their mutual challenges, the other guests may be neglected. Both the host and his guests should use some tact to bring about a change.

【 觞 政 （ 节 录 ） 】

清 · 沈中楹

登眺不宜尽醉，舟次不宜尽醉，坐有荆棘不宜尽醉，次日有要紧事不宜尽醉，乏舆从不宜尽醉，病初愈不宜尽醉。

主人罗列盘餐，竟无旨酒，稍减一二，加之酒上，何等合拍？

知己宴叙，快事也。有同席出令，漫不关心，一至当盆，错愕顾盼，以做不出三字评之。

设席先料客之不来，不曾全设，临坐客多席少，遂致上下差移，东西挨搭，可鄙之甚。

宾主尽欢，期于彼此各适。倘一味倾倒，久坐不散，使主家各役伺候，无不嗟怨，隆冬酷暑，更为不堪。

酒贵始终一色，有先淡后浓，或浓淡杂出，冷热不均，俱责以不恭之罪。

闯席一法，惟最相知始可。若孟浪概行，令人厌憎，同坐者常面面相觑，何不自爱？

平日往还，绝无杯酒，一当有事相求，忽多闹热周全，及至事后又复水冷，此等人不可与饮。

客或路远，或遇雨雪，或值夜禁，城门之隔，乃不约早坐，肴未全而星散，跟跄奔走，如此宴会，便不感激。

客未齐集，先有人剥削水果小菜，殊为不雅。但首席未到，主家不另为陪客点饥，枵腹坐待，毋怪乎渔猎以救荒也。

拳兴不知昉于何人，不过取其豪爽，若作奸作态，伸缩袅娜，丢拳夹马，品斯下矣。

侍从送酒合宜，善解令盆，良仆也。竟有面目可憎，山野不驯，盗酒窃肴，殊为障碍。

席间有妙令，无解人，有大量，无对手，亦为缺陷。

客有量小不能奉令，寄酒一斗，甚为两便。每见令官苛责，逼人呕吐狼藉，未免多事。

主人不劝客，不送骰色，客人不脱略，不肯行令，俱属闷酒，吾无取焉。

世情不等，每有沾沾责望报施，较量厚薄，竟似于饮食场中立命者，大雅讥之。

作客作主，不可太脱略，亦不必太拘泥。每有末坐犹然谦逊，使他客危立久候，更有肴馔甚薄，主人恣餐，使客无下箸处，大忌大忌。

同席人，异途开口敞治衙门，专说官府，秀才卖弄考第，此类均堪作景。

主人不能饮，须邀旁主大量才不寂寞。倘华筵专设，坐中冷气逼人，亦无趣味。

富贵人口头三昧，动称缺情，经年隔岁，无一践言。又有一种并无齿颊之殷殷，惟知趋饮之仆仆。二者病则一般。

共席或有同路，临散无相友之谊，更有水路舟楫，密密解维，不肯挈带，道眼鄙之。惟酒徒龌龊者避之可也。

对山人僧道，不宜另立边幅，诙谐取谑，既伤雅，亦取怨。

席间遇有村俗人品，切宜随缘安置，不可较长絜短，盖造物不齐，贤愚分定，有道气人自能包荒。

席间市语俚言，戈矛刺骨，或乘醉狂呼，酿成祸患，所当自重。

有一等人，风生四座，索酒索肴，遇着爽口适意之物，请益无厌，皆当省察。

联坐位次，须刻刻照顾界限，每有不亮左右之人，横开两臂，大肆牛饮，可憎也。

酒后语言颠倒，丑态备呈，甚有残肴仍置盘中，剩酒乱捐壶内，多带仆从，不惜主家，有养君子，不宜蹈此。

凡有吉凶之家，头绪纷纭，酒馔疏略，检点不周，均宜情亮。

诞日开筵，古人为母难日，或与稚子弥月周岁，尤当惜福，请戒杀生，功德无量。

移酌园亭，人多客杂，仆从折损花果，最为不近人情。

富贵之家，亲戚往来，常同陌路。及遇方外大头鬼，或阔帮闲，或盛名妓，美酒佳肴，流连不惜，此真贻谋之不灭也。

世情炎凉，当场逼露。如显贵同筵，趋承恐后，即多金村鄙，殷勤不怠。又有少年渺视父执，谈吐顾盼，绝不着意。均非明理人也。

酒席臭味不同，品类各别。有最惨而不觉者，如衙门公事酒，差役发纵，卖男鬻女，止供一时狂饮。又有最豪而不觉者，如败家荡子，声色狂迷，身命不顾，不可不深鉴戒。

酒令严如军令，有严而不能行，行而不能中节，使量大者无酒，量窄者苦酒，更有迷令之人，终席贸贸，皆严之不可为训者。

席尊专客，天性不饮，须耐烦终席，庶陪客尽欢。

凡婚嫁陪从，最忌酒徒，横生事端，有讼之家亦然。

监令之设，因客多不能专理，诚不可缺。乃有令官不举，强叼监令；监令已委，更来傍制叼监令，与监监令，均非至当。

请客难，速客更难。自午迄暮，速者胫折，望者眼穿，陪者腹枵，远者欲去，主人不能为情，同席不便先坐，大可闷事。

治席请陪客，专赖帮助主人，乃有先期相订。客已至而陪客未来，甚有迎合客欢，苛罚本家，此酒鬼不足道也。

昏暮客至，主人乏物，周旋掣肘，亦有一种说不出可厌处。

饮食宴乐，各宜得体。缙绅鄙啬，规模必不弘远；士庶奢靡，根器决难永固。不可不省。

宴新亲及童稚者，不宜说诗词故事，恐其语涩。

设席须称家有无。不可暴殄，不可落俗。设有应丰者而故俭之，不妨俭者而勉丰之，俱欠妥贴。

酒后许人馈赠或邀饮，相订凿凿，明旦尽成梦语，他日复尔。本人不觉，旁观意味索然。

偶尔茹素，默然赴席，及举箸虚拱，然后知为素客。众口苦劝，坚持不二，令主家措办不及，亦是作孽。

席上无人打酒官司，似觉寂寞。然专意打酒官司缠住一家，必有饮酒不均之怨矣。作客作主俱要随时变化。

Sound Mimicry

Preface to *Autumn Sounds* (*A Collection of Poems*)

Lin Tsehuan

c. 1650

During the autumn days, Che Aitzu [Lin Tsehuan] used to lock himself up indoors, and often he felt restless and did not know what to do. But whenever he heard of gossip and anecdotes, he dipped his pen in ink and wrote some poems. When these poems were collected together, he called them "autumn sounds." One day several of his friends dropped in to see him, and he asked them to stay and have a drink. He asked his guests to say what sounds they liked best respectively. "The sounds of the loom and the spinning wheel and of children reciting their lessons," said one of them. "What a good father!" said I. "The sounds of scolding footmen outside and of music and singing in the inner court," said another. "So you are given to luxuries," I commented. "The sounds of mother-in-law and daughter-

in-law playing chess," said a third. "How romantic!" A friend
who had remained hitherto silent, advanced with a large cup
filled with wine and said:

"May I tell you something you never heard of before? There is a
great imitator of sounds in the capital. On festive days, he sets
up a screen eight feet high in the northeastern corner of the
hall, and sits behind the screen with nothing except a table, a
chair, a fan, and a sounding board. The guests sit around. By
and by from behind the screen are heard two taps with the
sounding board, which is the signal for silence. At first, they
hear a dog barking far away in some alleyway. Then a woman
wakes up and yawns; she tries to wake up her husband and says
lewd things to him. The husband at first makes no reply but
mumbles in his sleep. The woman keeps on jerking him, when
the conversation between the two becomes clearer and clearer,
and there is a creaking of the bed. Then the baby wakes up. The
husband asks the woman to feed the baby, and while the baby
is sucking and crying, the woman pats the baby and coos it

to silence. Meanwhile, the husband has got up and is clearing himself, while the mother is also trying to make the baby urinate. This, however, wakes up the older child, who begins to cry vociferously. There is then started an immense confusion of sounds—of the woman patting the baby with her hand and cooing, the baby crying and sucking, the older child just waking up, the bed creaking, the husband scolding the older child, and the sounds of discharge in the night pot and the wooden pail. While the guests listen amazed with outstretched necks at this medley of realistic sounds, they hear the husband going to bed again. The wife then asks the older child to get up and clear himself also, and when this is done, they all get ready to go to sleep again. The baby is falling asleep. The husband begins to snore, and the rhythm of the wife patting her baby becomes slower and slower until it stops entirely. Then they hear a mouse going about the room and overturning things on the floor, while the woman coughs in her sleep. While the listeners begin to sit back and take it more easily, they suddenly hear a loud cry, 'Fire! Fire!' The husband gets up and shouts, the wife screams, and both children begin to cry. Very soon it seems there are hundreds of people shouting, hundreds of children crying, and hundreds of dogs barking, while through and above all this are heard the sounds of structures falling, fire cracking, wind blowing, water pouring, and men struggling and crying for help in a general pandemonium. The sounds are so real that the listeners' faces turn, their knees shake, and they almost take to their heels. But all of a sudden, a tap is heard and all sounds cease. When the screen is taken away, they see nothing but a table, a chair, a fan, and a sounding board."

Indeed here is a great painter of sounds. I set down my friend's words and let this serve as the preface to the *Autumn Sounds*.

【《秋声诗》自序】

清·林嗣环

彻呆子当正秋之日，杜门简出，毡有针，壁有衰甲，苦无可排解者。然每听谣诼之来，则濡墨呎笔而为诗。诗成，以"秋声"名篇。

适有数客至，不问何人，留共醉。酒酣，令客各举似何声最佳。一客曰："机声，儿子读书声佳耳。"予曰："何言之庄也？"又一客曰："堂下呵驺声，堂后笙歌声，何如？"予曰："何言之华也？"又一客曰："姑妇楸枰声最佳。"曰："何言之玄也？"一客独嘿嘿，乃取大杯满酌而前曰："先生喜闻人所未闻，仆请数言为先生抚掌，可乎？京中有善口技者。会宾客大宴，于厅事之东北角施八尺屏障，口技人坐屏障中，一桌、一椅、一扇、一抚尺而已。家宾团坐。少顷，但闻屏障中抚尺二下，满堂寂然，无敢哗者。遥遥闻深巷犬吠声，便有妇人惊觉欠伸，遥其夫语猥亵事。夫呓语，初不甚应。妇摇之不止，则二人语渐间杂，床又从中戛戛。既而儿醒大啼。夫令妇抚儿乳。儿含乳啼，妇拍而呜之。夫起溺，妇亦抱儿起溺。床上又一大儿醒，狺狺不止。当是时，妇手拍儿声，口中呜声，儿含乳啼声，大儿初醒声、床声、夫叱大儿声，溺瓶中声，溺桶中声，一齐凑发，众妙毕备。满座宾客，无不伸颈侧目，微笑嘿叹，以为妙绝也。既而夫上床寝，妇又呼大儿溺，毕，都上床寝。小儿亦渐欲睡，夫鼾声起，妇拍儿亦渐拍渐止。

微闻有鼠作作索索，盆器倾侧，妇梦中咳嗽之声。宾客意少舒，稍稍正坐。忽一人大呼火起。夫起大呼，妇亦起大呼，两儿齐哭。俄而百千人大呼，百千儿哭，百千犬吠。中间力拉崩倒之声，火爆声，呼呼风声，百千齐作。又夹百千求救声，曳屋许许声，抢夺声，泼水声。凡所应有，无所不有。虽人有百手，手有百指，不能指其一端；人有百口，口有百舌，不能名其一处也。于是宾客无不变色离席，奋袖出臂，两股战战，几欲先走。而忽然抚尺一下，群响毕绝，撤屏视之，一人、一桌、一椅、一扇、一抚尺而已！"

嘻！若而人者，可谓善画声矣！遂录其语，以为《秋声序》。

The Origin of Foot-binding

"A Note on Women's Shoes and Socks"

Yu Huai

1617-after 1697

Yu Huai is a connoisseur of inkstones and of women,
being best known for his volume on the singsong artists
of Yangchow. He places the origin of foot-binding at the
middle of the tenth century, while a commentator, Fei
Shihuang, wrote a postscript to dispute it, believing its
origin to be very much earlier. The case is not proven. What
is clear is that foot-binding became popular in the latter part
of the eleventh century. To make it easier to follow, it should
be noted that the distinctive characteristics of bound feet
with "bow shoes" are: (1) that in place of simple socks, long
bands of silk, perhaps seven or eight feet long, were used to
wind around the feet, and over these, a short embroidered
ankle cover was worn, (2) that such feet were reputed to
be very small, "three inches" being the goal, (3) that the
curved, pointed form of the feet was called the "crescent"
and the shoes were called "bow shoes." High heels alone, or
pointed and upturned fronts need not necessarily indicate
foot-binding. "Lotus steps" and "bamboo shoots" (round
and short and pointed at one end) are common expression,

and I think these do not always indicate the existence of foot-binding. The style probably originated in the licentious courts of certain rulers, the notorious "East Idiot Ruler" of South Tsi (c. A.D. 500) and the good-poet-but-bad-ruler Nantang Houtsu (reigned, A.D. 937-978), and became general custom later. In view of the exuberance of Tang poetry about women's beauty, its lack of specific reference to this curious custom should lead one to think that foot-binding was not yet the general custom in the Tang Period (seventh to ninth centuries). Yu Huai is probably correct.

There was no difference between the feet of women and of men in ancient times. The *Chouli* [classic on Chou governmental system] mentions the office of the "shoe man," whose duty was to look after the shoes of kings and queens. It mentions red clogs, black clogs, red and yellow silk braids, black curves, white shoes, linen shoes for formal, informal, and home use by the titled men and ladies. This shows that shoes of men and women were of the same form. In later generations, the small and slender bow shoes of women were prized for their smallness.

According to my research, foot-binding began with Li Houtsu of Nantang. He had a royal woman attendant called Yaoniang [Miss Yao], who was noted for her slender beauty and her dance. He had a golden lotus made, six feet high and decorated with precious stones and festoons and tassels of silk. This golden lotus in many colors stood in the center. He made Miss Yao tie her feet with silk and crouch on top of it to suggest the form of a crescent moon. She danced on top of the lotus in her white socks and made pirouettes suggesting the clouds [with her long sleeves]. Many people then began to copy her style. This was the first beginning of foot-binding.

This custom was not started before the Tang Dynasty (beginning A.D. 618). Therefore, among the poems written by so many poets singing the beauty of women, endlessly describing with great interest their looks and gestures, the richness of their hair ornaments and facial make-ups and their dresses and skirts, and the delicacy of their hair, eyes, lips, teeth, waists, and hands and wrists, not a word was said about their "small feet." In the *Kuyofu* [*Ancient Songs*] it says, "New silk embroidery covers her

white ankle and the arch of her feet was like a beautiful spring"
[Han Period]. Tsao Tsechien (A.D. 192-232) has a line which
reads, "She wears embroidered shoes for long walks." Li Po (A.D.
701-762) says in one poem, "A pair of gold-toothed clogs; two
feet white as frost." Han Chihkuang writes, "Six inches of fine
round skin dazzle in the light." Tu Muchih (A.D. 803-852) [a
great philanderer and poet] writes, "It measures one foot minus
four-tenths of an inch." The document "Miscellanies, Secret
H" of the second century says [describing a girl selected to be
queen], "Her feet measured eight inches, and her ankle and arch
were beautiful and full." Such mention of "six inches" and "eight
inches" of white, soft, and full feet shows that the ladies' feet
before Tang were not bent to resemble the crescent moon.

The case of the East Idiot Ruler of Tsi may come to mind.
He made his favorite royal concubine Miss Pan tread on gold
models of lotus flowers arranged on the floor, and said, "A gold
lotus flower arises from her every step." This, however, refers
to the models of lotus flowers which she trod upon, but is not

meant to say that her feet themselves were lotuses. Tsui Pao
mentions in his book on the origin of things, the *Kuchinchu*,
that there were phoenix-head shoes with double *tai* [soles?], but
there was no indication that only women's shoes were meant.

In the Sung Dynasty, few women bound their feet before the
reign of Yuanfeng (1078-1085). But in the almost four hundred
years that followed, beginning from the Mongol Dynasty
(1277-1367)[1] to the present, the unnatural fashions and
exaggerations have steadily grown and run into excesses.
Ancient women all wore socks. On the day that Queen Yang
Kueifei[2] died (c. A.D. 756) at Mahuai, a village woman picked
up half of a pair of her embroidered socks. She exhibited this

---

[1] Yuan Dynasty (1271-1368)——编者注。

[2] Probably the most famous, pampered, and extravagant queen of China's
history who almost brought an end to the Tang Dynasty. A revolt by her
lover, An Lushan, a Mongol or a Turk, caused the emperor to flee the capital.
The general public opinion had been so enraged by the extravagances of
her family that the army escorting the fleeing emperor refused to go farther
unless their demand to have the queen killed be complied with. She was
given a band of silk to hang herself with. Her corpse was shown to the
commanders and the army marched.

to the public, charging 100 cash for touching it. Li Po says in one of his poems, "Her feet are white as frost; she does not wear black-capped socks." One name for socks was *chiku* [ankle sheath]. When Emperor Kaotsung (reigned, 1127-1162) heard of the death of his prime minister, Tsin Kuei, he said, "Now I don't need to conceal a dagger in my *chiku*." Thus "socks" or *chiku* were worn by both men and women. The difference is that socks in ancient times had soles to them, as is not the case today. In ancient times, one could walk about in socks without shoes. Now we cannot.... Tsao Tsechien says, "She moves her light steps. Her silken socks become dusty." Li Houtsu writes, "She descends the perfumed steps in her socks, holding the gold-thread shoes in her hand." Such indeed is the difference in shoes and socks between the ancient and the modern times.

As to high heels, I do not find it mentioned in ancient books. This seems to be a modern invention. Some ladies of Wu make heels of sandalwood, covered with fine stiff silk. Some have carved heels, with a concealed perfume bag inside, so that they leave a trail of perfume as they walk about. This is a monstrous extravagance. I mention this because poems of the Sung and Mongol Dynasties made no reference to it, so that poets who want to write about ancient beauties should be careful on this point.

【 妇人鞋袜考 】

清·余怀

古妇人之足，与男子无异。《周礼》有屦人，掌王及后之服屦，为赤舄、黑舄、赤繶、黄繶、青勾素履、葛屦，辨外内命夫命妇之功屦、命屦、散屦。可见男女之履同一形制，非如后世女子之弓弯细纤，以小为贵也。考之缠足，起于南唐李后主。后主有宫嫔窅娘，纤丽善舞，乃命作金莲，高六尺，饰以珍宝，绷带缨络，中作品色瑞莲，令窅娘以帛缠足，屈上作新月状，着素袜，行舞莲中，回旋有凌云之态。由是人多效之，此缠足所自始也。唐以前未开此风，故词客诗人，歌咏美人好女，容态之殊丽，颜色之天姣，以至面妆首饰、衣褶裙裾之华靡，鬓发、眉目、唇齿、腰肢、手腕之阿娜秀洁，无不津津乎其言之，而无一语及足之纤小者。即如古乐府之《双行缠》云："新罗绣白胫，足趺如春妍。"曹子建云："践远游之文履"，李太白诗云："一双金齿屐，两足白如霜。"韩致光诗云："六寸肤圆光致致"，杜牧之诗云："钿尺裁量减四分"，汉《杂事秘辛》云："足长八寸，胫跗丰妍。"夫六寸八寸，素白丰妍，可见唐以前妇人之足，无屈上作新月状者也。即东昏潘妃，作金莲花帖地，令妃行其上，曰"此步步生金莲花"，非谓足为金莲也。崔豹《古今注》："东晋有凤头重台之履"，不专言妇人也。宋元丰以前，缠足者尚少，自元至今将四百年，矫揉造作亦泰甚矣。古妇人皆着袜。杨太真死之日，马嵬媪得锦䩙袜一只，过客一玩百钱。李太白诗云："溪上足如霜，不着鸦头袜。"袜一名"膝裤"。宋高宗闻秦桧死，喜曰："今后免膝裤中插匕首矣。"则袜也，膝裤也，乃男女之通称，原无分别。但古有底，今无底耳。古有底之袜，不必着鞋，皆可行地；今无底之袜，非着鞋，则寸步不能行矣。张平子云："罗袜凌蹑足容与"。曹子建云："凌波微步，罗袜生尘。"李后主词云："划袜下香阶，手提金缕鞋。"古今鞋袜之制，其不同如此。至于高底之制，前古未闻，于今独绝。吴下妇人，有以异香为底，围以精绫者；有凿花玲珑，囊以香麝，行步霏霏，印香在地者。此则服妖，宋元以来诗人所未及，故表而出之，以告世之赋"香奁"，咏"玉台"者。

The Ferryman's Wisdom

From *Prose Works of Chou Yung*

Chou Yung

1619-1679

> Like many great painters during the Ming Dynasty, Chou
> Yung was one of the many poets whose disappointment at
> the Manchu conquest made them seek their escape, and
> find their salvation, in poetry and painting. It was said that
> "his painting was better than his prose, his poems better
> than his paintings, and his calligraphy better than his
> poems." He refused to accept office in the government.

In the winter of 1650, I was going into the city of Chiaochuan
from the Little Harbor, accompanied by a boy carrying a big
load of books, tied with a cord and strengthened with a few
pieces of board.

It was toward sunset and the country was covered with haze.

We were about a mile from the city.

"Will we be in time to get into the city before the gates are closed?" I asked the ferryman.

"You will if you go slowly. But if you run, you will miss it," replied the ferryman, casting a look at the boy.

But we walked as fast as possible. About halfway, the boy fell down. The cord broke and the books fell on the ground. The boy sat crying. By the time we had retied the package and reached the city gate, it was already closed.

I thought of that ferryman. He had wisdom.

【 小港渡者 】

清·周容

　　庚寅冬，予自小港欲入蛟川城，命小奚以木简束书从。时西日沉山，晚烟萦树，望城二里许，因问渡者："尚可得南门开否？"渡者熟视小奚，应曰："徐行之尚开也，速进则阖。"予愠为戏。趋行及半，小奚仆，束断书崩，啼未即起。理书就束而前，门已牡下矣。予爽然思渡者言近道。天下之以躁急自败，穷暮而无所归宿者，其犹是也夫，其犹是也夫！

無邊落木蕭蕭下
不盡長江滾滾來

清·王时敏　杜甫诗意图

On City Noises

Sha Changpai

c. 1671

There are noises of the forests, of the jungles, and of the cities. When birds, beasts, and men get together, one always hears a booming, boiling confusion of noises. Sometimes one listens to the cries of animals and songs of birds in the forests and imagines that these cries and songs are pure expressions of joy without a purpose. By the analogy of human noises in the city, however, one must conclude that they have a very definite purpose, either to show off what they have got, or to cry for what they haven't, for the satisfaction of some immediate primitive desires.

The climate of Peking is dry, and the city noises carry a long way. The peddlers' cries are heard everywhere, on the avenues, in the alleys, and in the most remote areas. The peddlers carry their wares and thread the streets where homes are to sell what the housewives may want to buy. There are thousands of them, in rain or shine, morning and night. These noises are noises of men who have something to sell and want to sell it. It would be unreasonable to assume that the noises of men are for the satisfaction of some needs and those of animals are not. I think of these cries as cries of men who cry aloud and appeal to the public that they have something to sell in order that they may make a living thereby, and who continue to do so till the end of their days.

This noise of the city is therefore symbolic of all human activities and professions. All mankind tries to sell something. Those who have power sell power and those who have influence sell influence. Artists, writers, officials, bureaucrats, and women sell their art, their writing, their favors, their cunning and thought and personal charms to obtain what they want. They all try to show off what they have got, and cry for what they haven't, for the satisfaction of some immediate desires. There are even whispers in the middle of the night, and caucuses behind closed doors, on unmentionable topics and inaudible to the world outside, the words without noise, the song without words, for the satisfaction of some immediate needs, which speak nevertheless louder than the bells and drums of the city. The function of these noiseless noises is the same as that of peddlers' cries, but the contents are not always so honorable.

Alas! only the phoenix can command the harmony of the birds' songs, only the unicorn can bring order to the cries of animals, and only the sages can bring about the satisfaction of men's needs so that the voice of men shall be a voice of peace and happiness, not a voice of turmoil and discontent. It is not right that men should escape to the mountains and live as hermits to enjoy the songs of birds and cries of animals, thus placing men below the animal creation.

【 市声说 】

清·沙张白

鸟之声聚于林，兽之声聚于山，人之声聚于市。是声也，盖无在无之，而当其所聚，则尤为庞杂沸腾，令听者难为聪焉。今人入山林者闻鸟兽之声，以为是天籁适然，鸣其自乐之致而已。由市声推之，乌知彼羽毛之族非多求多冀，哓哓焉炫其所有，急其所无，以求济夫旦夕之欲者乎！

京师土燥水涩，其声噌以呿，鬻百货于市者类为曼声高呼，夸所挟以求售。肩任担负，络绎孔道，至于穷墟僻巷，无所不到，传呼之声相闻，盖不知几千万人也！祁寒暑雨莫不自晨迄暮，不肯少休，抗喉而疾呼，以求济其旦夕之欲耳！苟谓鸟之呼于林，兽之呼于山者，皆怡然自得，一无所求。而人者独否，是天之恩勤群类，予以自然之乐者，反丰于物而靳于人，此亦理之不可信者也。然使此千百万人者厌其勤苦，且自悔不鸟兽若，尽弃其业而他业焉，将京师之大，阒然寂然，不特若曹无以赡其生，生民之所需畴为给之！此又势之必不可者矣！顾使其中有数人焉，耻其所为而从吾所好，则为圣贤，为仙佛，为贵人，为高士，何不可者！吾惜其自少至老日疾为抗喉疾呼，而皇皇于道路以死也。甚矣，市声之可哀也！

清·沈源 灯市行图

虽然，市者声之所聚，京师者又市之所聚也。揽权者市权，挟势者市势，以至市文章、市技艺、市恩、市诌、市诈、市面首、市颦笑，无非市者炫其所有，急其所无，汲汲然求济其旦夕之欲。虽不若市声之哓哓然，而无声之声震于钟鼓矣！甚且暮夜之乞怜无声，中庭之相泣有声，反不若抗声捷呼者之为其事而不讳其名也。君子之所哀岂仅在市声也哉！

嗟乎！有凤凰焉，而后可以和百鸟之声；有麒麟焉，而后可以谐百兽之声；有圣人焉，而后能使天下之人之声皆得其中，终和且平，而无噍杀嚣凌之患。四灵不至，君子所为致慨也。若曰厌苦人声而欲逃之山林，以听夫无所求而自然之鸣焉，是鸟兽同群而薄斯人之吾与也。

Some Dog Stories

From *Yutsu Shinchih*

Wang Yen

17th century

> These dog stories, preserved in the collection *Yutsu Shinchih* edited by Chang Chao with a preface dated 1683, were called in their original title *Our Animal Teachers*. There are always wise souls who believe that the animals have a lot to teach us, and there are always open-minded persons who can see that man is the most degenerate of all animals and that a healthy return to original simplicity of character may be the salvation of mankind. It is in this sense that Wang Yen calls animals not only our teachers but "saint-teachers." This collection consists chiefly of the editor's contemporaries and the author is presumed to have lived in the seventeenth century.

In the time of Sun Wu during the Three Kingdoms (third century) there was a Chi Hsinshun who kept a dog, called "Black Dragon." Black Dragon followed him wherever he went. One day Chi was dead drunk and lay down to sleep on a patch of wild grass outside the city. It happened that an officer was out hunting and had caused a fire in the wild tract. Black Dragon, sensing the danger, tried to wake him up and tugged at his gown, but without avail. He saw there was a little creek about thirty yards from the place, went to the creek, and dipped himself in the water. Then he came back and rolled on the grass where his master was still lying in heavy slumber. The dog kept on repeating this operation, running through the smoke and fire, until the little patch of grass was thoroughly wet. The dog was burned himself and died. He had, however, succeeded in saving the master, and when the latter woke up, he saw Black Dragon lying dead by his side, the place all wet and the rest of the patch all burned up. He realized what Black Dragon had done for him and wept bitterly. Out of a sense of gratitude, he petitioned the magistrate, and gave the dog a regular human burial, with a coffin and proper burial gowns. Now there is still a mound at Chinan, called "the Tomb of the Righteous Dog."

Yuan Tsan died as a revolutionist. He left a three-year-old orphan, and his amah brought him to the home of one of Yuan's students, by the name of Ti Lingching. This Ti was a rascal and said, "I hear there is a reward for anyone who delivers Yuan's orphan." The amah was furious and protested: "I have come to you with this orphan because you owe debts of gratitude to your master. If you kill this baby to obtain the reward, you will one day die an untimely death. The gods will avenge your master." The child was killed in spite of the amah's protest. Now the child had a big, hairy dog as his friend, and used to ride on the dog while at play. A year after the child died, a big dog suddenly appeared at Ti's home, met him in the yard, and bit him to death. Then he went in and bit Ti's wife also. This was the dog that the child used to play with.

General Chi Chiung of Tang Dynasty used to keep four big hunting dogs who accompanied him on his hunting trips. The general fed them with meat, and noticed that one of them always took a piece in his mouth and ran out to a hidden bush to eat it and would then return. Piqued by curiosity, Chi ordered a servant to follow the dog to the bush. The servant found that the dog had an old, sick mother, thin, emaciated, and diseased. Struck by the dog's conduct, Chi had the mother dog brought home and fed properly, while her son would look on and wag his tail in happiness and gratitude. Thereafter, the dog proved his gratitude by being always the first to catch the game. A year afterward, the mother dog died, and the dog felt upset for days. Later on, when Chi died, the dog watched over his coffin during the entire funeral ceremonies, and when the coffin was let into the ground, the dog scratched the ground madly and died before the grave was completed.

A certain Chang of Kueichi had to go abroad, leaving in his home only his young wife and a man servant. In time, the two did the logical thing under the circumstances. Chang had a dog by the name of "Black Dragon" who accompanied him abroad. When master and dog returned, the servant and mistress plotted to kill him. A dinner was prepared, and while they sat around the board, pretending to celebrate his return, Chang had discovered the plot and sat silently at the table. He threw a piece of meat to the dog and said, "I have kept you for so many years. Now I am in danger of life. Save me." The dog looked at the meat and then at the servant. Chang slapped his thigh and cried: "Black Dragon!" Thereupon the dog leapt upon the servant, who, taken by surprise, dropped his knife to the ground and fell down, and the dog bit off his genitals. Chang then took the knife and killed the servant. His wife was sent to prison and sentenced to death.

During the rebellion of Yang Kuangyuan at Chingchow, there was a Mr. Sun living in the city. The food supply was running short in the besieged city, and there was no way of obtaining food from his villa in the country. While the family did not know what to do, they saw their dog lying by the master's side and looking at them wistfully. "Can you go to the villa and fetch food for me?" Sun asked the dog, and the dog wagged his tail as if he understood. At night they attached a bag on the dog's neck with a letter in it and the dog left the city through a water gate. Arriving at his master's villa, the dog kept barking until he was admitted. Learning the message contained in the letter, they sent the dog back with a bag of rice. This was kept up for several months until the siege was called off. For this reason, the whole family was grateful to the dog for saving their lives. When the dog died several years afterward, they buried him in a beautiful spot in the villa.

【 圣师录（节录） 】

清·王言

孙吴时，襄阳纪信纯，一犬名乌龙，行住相随。一日，城外大醉，归家不及，卧草中。太守邓瑕出猎，纵火爇草，犬以口衔纯衣，不动。有溪相去三五十步，犬入水湿身，来卧处周回，以身湿之。火至湿处即灭。犬困乏，致毙于侧。信纯获免，醒见犬死毛湿，观火踪迹，因而痛哭。闻于太守，命具棺衾葬之。今纪南有"义犬冢"，高十余丈。

袁粲值萧道成将革命，自以身受顾托，谋起义，遂遇害。有儿方数岁，乳母携投粲门生狄灵庆。庆曰："吾闻出郎君者厚赏。"乳母号呼曰："公昔有恩于汝，故冒难归汝。若杀郎君以求利，神明有知，行见汝族灭也！"儿竟死。儿存时，尝骑一大氅狗戏。死后年余，忽有狗入庆家，遇庆入庭，啮杀之，并其妻。即向所骑狗也。

清·郎世宁 十骏犬图之金翅猃

唐禁军大校齐琼，家畜良犬四，常畋回广囿，辄饲以粱肉。其一独填茹咽喉齿牙间以出，如隐丛薄，然后食，食已，则复至。齐窃异之，一日令仆伺其所往，则北垣枯窦，有母存焉，老瘠疥秽，吐哺以饲。齐奇叹久之，乃命篚牝犬归，以败茵席之，余饼饵饱之。犬则摇尾俯首，若怀知感。尔后擒奸逐狡，指顾如飞将，扈猎驾前，必获丰赏。逾年牝死，犬加勤效。后齐卒，犬日夜嗥吠。越月，将有事于邱陇，则留犬以御奸盗。及悬棺之夕，犬独来，足蹄土成拗，首叩棺见血。掩土未毕，犬亦至毙。

会稽张然滞役，有少妇无子，惟与一奴守舍，奴遂与妇通焉。然素养一犬，名"乌龙"，常以自随。后归，奴欲谋杀然，盛作饮食。妇曰："与君当大别离，君可强啖！"奴已张弓拔矢，须然食毕。然涕泣不能食，以肉及饭掷狗，祝曰："养汝经年，吾当将死，汝能救我否？"犬得食，不啖，惟注眼视奴。然拍膝大呼曰："乌龙！"犬应声伤奴。奴失刀遂倒，狗咋其阴。然因取刀杀奴，以妻付县杀之。

杨光远叛于青州，有孙中舍居围城中，族在西州别墅。城闭久，食尽，举家愁叹。犬彷徨其侧，似有忧思。中舍因嘱曰："尔能为我至庄取米耶？"犬摇尾若应状。至夜，置一布囊，并简系犬背上。犬由水窦出，至庄鸣吠。居者开门，识其犬，取简视之，令负米还。如此数月，以至城开。孙氏阖门，赖以不馁，愈爱畜此犬。后数年毙，葬于别墅。至其孙彭年，语龙图赵师民，刻石表其墓，曰"灵犬志"。

编后记

《林语堂英译诗文选》丛书共分六册，英汉双语形式呈现，诗文书画相映成趣。篇目摘自林语堂 *The Importance of Understanding*（《古文小品译英》）、*The Gay Genius: Life and Times of Su Tungpo*（《苏东坡传》）、*The Wisdom of China and India*（《中国印度之智慧》）等著作。丛书编辑过程中，具有时代特色的英文行文一概存旧，除林语堂英文原注外，补充若干编者注，并附中文诗文，供读者参考。

美国波士顿大学艺术史系白谦慎教授为各分册题写书名，杭州师范大学江平副教授为附图提供指导，谨致谢忱。

京权图字：01-2007-1904

图书在版编目（CIP）数据

明清小品. 上：英、汉 / 林语堂著. — 北京：外语教学与研究出版社，2015.2（2016.12 重印）
（林语堂英译诗文选）
ISBN 978-7-5135-5629-3

Ⅰ. ①明… Ⅱ. ①林… Ⅲ. ①小品文 - 作品集 - 中国 - 明清时代 - 英、汉 Ⅳ. ①I264.8

中国版本图书馆CIP数据核字（2015）第042135号

出 版 人　蔡剑峰
书名题签　白谦慎
系列策划　吴　浩
责任编辑　段会香
装帧设计　覃一彪
出版发行　外语教学与研究出版社
社　　址　北京市西三环北路19号（100089）
网　　址　http://www.fltrp.com
印　　刷　北京华联印刷有限公司
开　　本　787×1092　1/32
印　　张　9.5
版　　次　2015年5月第1版 2016年12月第2次印刷
书　　号　ISBN 978-7-5135-5629-3
定　　价　66.00元

购书咨询：（010）88819926　电子邮箱：club@fltrp.com
外研书店：https://waiyants.tmall.com
凡印刷、装订质量问题，请联系我社印制部
联系电话：（010）61207896　电子邮箱：zhijian@fltrp.com
凡侵权、盗版书籍线索，请联系我社法律事务部
举报电话：（010）88817519　电子邮箱：banquan@fltrp.com
法律顾问：立方律师事务所　刘旭东律师
　　　　　中咨律师事务所　殷　斌律师
物料号：256290001